OPPOSING
VIEWPOINTS®
SERIES

The Power of Protest

Other Books of Related Interest

Opposing Viewpoints Series

Black Lives Matter
Cancel Culture
Labor Unions and Workers' Rights
The #MeToo Movement
Western Democracy at Risk

At Issue Series

Athlete Activism
Is America a Democracy or an Oligarchy?
Partisanship
Public Outrage and Protest
When Is Free Speech Hate Speech?

Current Controversies Series

Antifa and the Radical Left
Attacks on Science
Freedom of Speech on Campus
Historical Revisionism
Microaggressions, Safe Spaces, and Trigger Warnings

> "Congress shall make no law ... abridging the freedom of speech, or of the press."

First Amendment to the US Constitution

The basic foundation of our democracy is the First Amendment guarantee of freedom of expression. The Opposing Viewpoints series is dedicated to the concept of this basic freedom and the idea that it is more important to practice it than to enshrine it.

OPPOSING
VIEWPOINTS®
SERIES

| The Power of Protest

Avery Elizabeth Hurt, Book Editor

GREENHAVEN
PUBLISHING

Published in 2023 by Greenhaven Publishing, LLC
29 East 21st Street
New York, NY 10010

Articles in Greenhaven Publishing anthologies are often edited for length to meet page
requirements. In addition, original titles of these works are changed to clearly present
the main thesis and to explicitly indicate the author's opinion. Every effort is made to
ensure that Greenhaven Publishing accurately reflects the original intent of the authors.
Every effort has been made to trace the owners of the copyrighted material.

Cover image: Halfpoint/Shutterstock.com.

Library of Congress Cataloging-in-Publication Data

Names: Hurt, Avery Elizabeth, editor.
Title: The power of protest / Avery Elizabeth Hurt, book editor.
Description: First Edition. | New York : Greenhaven Publishing, LLC, 2023.
 | Series: Opposing Viewpoints | Includes bibliographical references and
 index. | Audience: Ages 15+ years | Audience: Grades 10–12 | Summary:
 "Anthology of essays examining the effectiveness of public protests in
 driving change, the need for leadership, social media's impact on
 protest, and whether violence is ever acceptable"— Provided by
 publisher.
Identifiers: LCCN 2021055650 | ISBN 9781534508774 (Library Binding) | ISBN
 9781534508767 (Paperback)
Subjects: LCSH: Political participation—United States—Juvenile
 literature. | Protest movements—United States—History—Juvenile
 literature. | Student movements—United States—History—Juvenile
 literature. | Nonviolence—Juvenile literature.
Classification: LCC JK1764 .P679 2023 | DDC 323/.0420973—dc23/eng/20220206
LC record available at https://lccn.loc.gov/2021055650

Manufactured in the United States of America

Website: http://greenhavenpublishing.com

Contents

Chapter 4: Has Social Media Helped Make Protest Movements More Effective?

The Importance of Opposing Viewpoints

P erhaps every generation experiences a period in time in which the populace seems especially polarized, starkly divided on the important issues of the day and gravitating toward the far ends of the political spectrum and away from a consensus-facilitating middle ground. The world that today's students are growing up in and that they will soon enter into as active and engaged citizens is deeply fragmented in just this way. Issues relating to terrorism, immigration, women's rights, minority rights, race relations, health care, taxation, wealth and poverty, the environment, policing, military intervention, the proper role of government—in some ways, perennial issues that are freshly and uniquely urgent and vital with each new generation—are currently roiling the world.

If we are to foster a knowledgeable, responsible, active, and engaged citizenry among today's youth, we must provide them with the intellectual, interpretive, and critical-thinking tools and experience necessary to make sense of the world around them and of the all-important debates and arguments that inform it. After all, the outcome of these debates will in large measure determine the future course, prospects, and outcomes of the world and its peoples, particularly its youth. If they are to become successful members of society and productive and informed citizens, students need to learn how to evaluate the strengths and weaknesses of someone else's arguments, how to sift fact from opinion and fallacy, and how to test the relative merits and validity of their own opinions against the known facts and the best possible available information. The landmark series Opposing Viewpoints has been providing students with just such critical-thinking skills and exposure to the debates surrounding society's most urgent contemporary issues for many years, and it continues to serve this essential role with undiminished commitment, care, and rigor.

The key to the series's success in achieving its goal of sharpening students' critical-thinking and analytic skills resides in its title—

Opposing Viewpoints. In every intriguing, compelling, and engaging volume of this series, readers are presented with the widest possible spectrum of distinct viewpoints, expert opinions, and informed argumentation and commentary, supplied by some of today's leading academics, thinkers, analysts, politicians, policy makers, economists, activists, change agents, and advocates. Every opinion and argument anthologized here is presented objectively and accorded respect. There is no editorializing in any introductory text or in the arrangement and order of the pieces. No piece is included as a "straw man," an easy ideological target for cheap point-scoring. As wide and inclusive a range of viewpoints as possible is offered, with no privileging of one particular political ideology or cultural perspective over another. It is left to each individual reader to evaluate the relative merits of each argument—as he or she sees it, and with the use of ever-growing critical-thinking skills—and grapple with his or her own assumptions, beliefs, and perspectives to determine how convincing or successful any given argument is and how the reader's own stance on the issue may be modified or altered in response to it.

This process is facilitated and supported by volume, chapter, and selection introductions that provide readers with the essential context they need to begin engaging with the spotlighted issues, with the debates surrounding them, and with their own perhaps shifting or nascent opinions on them. In addition, guided reading and discussion questions encourage readers to determine the authors' point of view and purpose, interrogate and analyze the various arguments and their rhetoric and structure, evaluate the arguments' strengths and weaknesses, test their claims against available facts and evidence, judge the validity of the reasoning, and bring into clearer, sharper focus the reader's own beliefs and conclusions and how they may differ from or align with those in the collection or those of their classmates.

Research has shown that reading comprehension skills improve dramatically when students are provided with compelling, intriguing, and relevant "discussable" texts. The subject matter of these collections could not be more compelling, intriguing, or urgently relevant to today's students and the world they are poised to inherit. The anthologized articles and the reading and discussion questions that are included with them also provide the basis for stimulating, lively, and passionate classroom debates. Students who are compelled to anticipate objections to their own argument and identify the flaws in those of an opponent read more carefully, think more critically, and steep themselves in relevant context, facts, and information more thoroughly. In short, using discussable text of the kind provided by every single volume in the Opposing Viewpoints series encourages close reading, facilitates reading comprehension, fosters research, strengthens critical thinking, and greatly enlivens and energizes classroom discussion and participation. The entire learning process is deepened, extended, and strengthened.

For all of these reasons, Opposing Viewpoints continues to be exactly the right resource at exactly the right time—when we most need to provide readers with the critical-thinking tools and skills that will not only serve them well in school but also in their careers and their daily lives as decision-making family members, community members, and citizens. This series encourages respectful engagement with and analysis of opposing viewpoints and fosters a resulting increase in the strength and rigor of one's own opinions and stances. As such, it helps make readers "future ready," and that readiness will pay rich dividends for the readers themselves, for the citizenry, for our society, and for the world at large.

Introduction

> *"Every man of humane convictions must decide on the protest that best suits his convictions, but we must all protest."*
>
> Dr. Martin Luther King Jr.

W hen you think of political or social protest, what comes to mind? Today it might well be the Black Lives Matter movement. A decade ago, you may have thought of Occupy Wall Street. A generation ago, it would likely have been the protest movement against the Vietnam War, and before that, the civil rights movement. But protest wasn't born in the twentieth century, though—at least in the United States. The years since Rosa Parks refused to give up her bus seat have been filled with many citizen actions and protests. However, a close look at history shows protests are nothing new.

In 1381, English peasants revolted against the class structure in place at that time, demanding equality for all. This revolt was not a success in the short term—a crackdown followed—but it was an early indication of the end of the feudal system in England. A more familiar protest might be the one that took place in Boston in 1773: the Boston Tea Party. Colonists' cry of "no taxation without representation" became the motto of the American Revolution, and we know how that ended. In 1778, the French people rose up against their leaders with the cry "liberty, equality, fraternity," a phrase that is now the motto of France. In 1791, inspired by the French Revolution, enslaved people in Haiti revolted against their oppressors, beginning one of the most successful slave revolts in history and leading to the establishment of the first Black republic.

In 1911, a revolution against China's imperial rulers led to the establishment of the Republic of China. In 1917, the Russian people overthrew Tsar Nicolas II. Protesters, led by Mahatma Gandhi, booted British colonizers out of India and drove the establishment of an independent Indian state in 1947.

And these are just the big ones. Over the centuries, protesters have demanded better wages and better working conditions, the right to vote, LGBTQ rights, prison reform, peace, an end to abortion, protection of the right to abortion, the right of girls to an education, immigration reform, tax reform, and dozens of other demands. Often protesters have changed their societies, and sometimes the world. But not always.

In a photograph taken at the 2017 Women's March, an older woman can be seen holding a sign that reads, "I can't believe I'm still having to protest this sh**." Many would say that protests gave us the Civil Rights Act, ended the Vietnam War, freed India from British rule, earned women the right to vote, and gained better wages for farmworkers. Others, feeling much like the woman at the Women's March, point out that protesting injustice is a never-ending job. The 1964 Civil Rights Act was gutted by a Supreme Court decision in 2013. Women won the right to vote, but despite being a majority in the nation, their health and reproductive rights are constantly imperiled. And the Vietnam War was ended, some say, not because of protests, but because of other causes such as cost and lack of discipline in the military. Looking at all this, one may ask the question: Do protests even work?

And what is the most effective way to protest? Is nonviolent protest more successful than violent resistance? Nonviolent protests as led by Mahatma Gandhi and Martin Luther King Jr. are usually seen as exemplars of protest movements. But not all campaigners agree that nonviolence is the best approach. When the opposition is willing to kill protesters, what is the point of remaining violence-free, they ask. And even some of those who are committed to the principle of nonviolence point out that it can be very difficult in the heat of the action to keep a protest peaceful. Yet, some say that for a cause to have moral authority, it must remain peaceful—and the way to keep protests peaceful is to have strong, charismatic leadership demonstrating and demanding that approach. However, in today's protest movements, leadership looks very different than it did a generation ago.

Great leaders, such as King and Gandhi and labor leader Cesar Chavez, have been the faces of protest movements in the past. Today, however, most movements lack one charismatic leader as the face of the cause. Protests are decentralized, and leadership is often local. Even at the local level, movements are more likely to be led by groups and coalitions than by a single individual.

Protests may not be new, but modern protests have some very new tools. Social media was particularly useful in the Arab Spring protests and is a hallmark of the Black Lives Matter movement. Social media is relatively new, so it remains to be seen how it contributes to or hinders protest movements. It is extremely effective in terms of awareness and mobilizing, but it has not proven to be as successful at implementing action.

Opposing Viewpoints: The Power of Protest starts with the premise that as long as people are being oppressed, some will be bold enough to take to the streets and protest that oppression. In chapters titled "Do Protests Work?" "Are Peaceful Protests More Effective Than Violent Protests?" "Do Protest Movements Require Charismatic Leaders?" and "Has Social Media Helped Make Protest Movements More Effective?" viewpoint authors discuss what works and what doesn't when it comes to mounting a successful protest in the face of injustice.

CHAPTER 1

Do Protests Work?

Chapter Preface

P rotest movements have often been given the credit for tremendous social and political change. Yet the results of those protests are not always clear. Some would say that protests against the US involvement in the Vietnam War ended the presidency of Lyndon Johnson, and may have, eventually, brought an end to that war. Others say the events that led to the US leaving Vietnam are far more complicated. Other protests have had ambiguous results. The movement that came to be known as the Arab Spring did not lead to the lasting change protesters and supporters hoped for. Today, we see the growth of the Black Lives Matter movement as well as other actions for social and economic justice and democracy around the world. We can't say yet if these movements will have a lasting effect, though they have clearly contributed to some change already.

The viewpoint authors in this chapter address the question of how effective protests are in securing progress and change and calling governments to account. The first viewpoint looks at the Arab Spring and sees, if not success, then reason for hope. The second points out that protests are effective, otherwise why would they get so much push-back from opponents of their causes? On the other hand, says another author, if protests work then why do campaigners keep fighting the same battles over and over? In answer to that, several young activists lay out the techniques protesters need to adopt if they want their campaigns to result in lasting change. Protests *can* work, these authors write, but they must be carefully managed. The final viewpoint of this chapter examines how protests can effect political parties and election outcomes.

> *"The US and Europe had, and continue to have, a vested interest in maintaining the anti-democratic status quo in most of the region."*

The Arab Spring Didn't Result in Lasting Change—but There's Still Hope

Finian Cunningham

In 2011, a series of events known as the Arab Spring gave hope to supporters of democracy in the Middle East and elsewhere. However, the changes did not last—or at least didn't result in the permanent, sweeping change protesters hoped for. In the following viewpoint, Finian Cunningham argues that Western governments have intentionally and successfully supported anti-democratic regimes in order to protect capitalist institutions. However, he writes, there is always hope for change, and the revolutions are not over. Finian Cunningham is an award-winning journalist who specializes in international affairs.

As you read, consider the following questions:

1. Why does the author say that Washington likely did not engineer the Arab Spring revolts?
2. What instead was the motivation for the revolts?
3. What does Cunningham mean when he says there is hope for a European and American Spring?

"The Arab Spring: Restoration, Repression & Regime Change," by Finian Cunningham, Strategic Culture Foundation, January 22, 2018. Reprinted by permission.

The outbreak of mass protests in Tunisia this week comes on the seventh anniversary of the Arab Spring uprisings in 2011. This week, seven years ago, saw Tunisia's strongman ruler Ben Ali fleeing for exile to Saudi Arabia. Before the month was out, Egypt's longtime ruler Hosni Mubarak was also ousted. Back then, revolution was in the air and the region was convulsed with potential change. In many ways, arguably, it still is.

Seven years on it is appropriate that social protests have reemerged in Tunisia. That demonstrates the Arab Spring is still unfinished business. The potential change for full democracy did not occur back then, nor since. At least, not yet.

Tunisia was the first country where the uprisings in 2011 kicked off after a young street vendor named Mohamed Bouazizi self-immolated in protest against poverty and state corruption. Today, protesters in Tunisia are still calling for liberation from political and economic oppression.

So, we may ask, what happened the Arab Spring and its promise for sweeping progressive change?

Before we review the momentous events, a note of clarification is needed. Back in the heyday of the Arab Spring some analysts posited that the social movements were part of a grand plan orchestrated by Washington to clear out despots who had passed their sell-by dates. Authors like Michel Chossudovsky and William Engdahl were among those claiming a hidden hand from Washington as part of a grand scheme. They point to communications between the State Department and certain protester groups, like the April 6 youth movement in Egypt, as evidence of a master-scheme manipulated from Washington. In that view, the Arab Spring was just another version of so-called Color Revolutions, which Washington did indeed orchestrate in other parts of the world, like Georgia and Ukraine in the early 2000s.

This author disagrees on what was the motive force behind the Arab Spring events. Admittedly, Washington did have a hand in the events, but more often this was reactionary, to curtail and divert the mass uprisings—uprisings which in this author's observations were genuine popular revolts against the US and European-backed status quo serving international capital.

Instead of successful revolution, what happened the Arab Spring were three categories of reaction. Here we look at seven countries in the region to illustrate.

Restoration

Tunisians and Egyptians may have seen the backs of Ben Ali and Mubarak, but seven years on it is evident that the ruling system that both these strongmen oversaw has been restored. In Tunisia, the Nidaa Tounes party that Ben Ali patronized is in power as part of a coalition with the Nahda Islamist party. The ruling structure of crony capitalism remains in place. The government's signing up to an IMF loan last year for $2.9 billion is conditioned on imposing harsh economic austerity cuts on the majority working-class population. The rule of international capital has thus been restored.

In Egypt, the Mubarak regime was restored through Abdel Fattah el-Sisi ousting Mohamed Morsi in July 2013. El-Sisi was a senior military holdover from Mubarak's 30-year de facto dictatorship. Admittedly, Morsi's ascent to power after Mubarak did not represent a pluralist democratic revolution. Morsi was beholden to the Muslim Brotherhood and his short-lived rule was associated with disturbing sectarian hostility. His government alienated secular Egyptian workers. Nevertheless, el-Sisi's violent overthrow of Morsi can be seen as a reactionary restoration of the old regime. Like Tunisia, today Egypt resembles much of the status quo as before the 2011 uprisings.

Repression

Three countries illustrating this category are Saudi Arabia, Bahrain and Yemen. There were similar developments in other countries, such as Jordan, Oman, Morocco, but on a smaller scale.

After Ben Ali and Mubarak fled from power, the Arab Spring wave soon buffeted Saudi Arabia, Bahrain and Yemen. Like Tunisia and Egypt, those three countries were ruled by US-backed despots.

If the whole regional ferment was somehow a devious plot to renovate the status quo by Washington, as some authors contended, then why didn't the despots in Saudi Arabia and Bahrain succumb to the State Department's "human rights" proxies?

This author was in Bahrain when its protests erupted on February 14, 2011. For almost one month, the Al Khalifa monarchial regime was reeling from mortal insecurity. The protests were mainly led by the majority Shia population against the Sunni self-styled king. Their demands, as far as this author observed, were for a worker-dedicated democracy, not a sectarian Islamic-style revolution. Bahrain's protests were brutally repressed with the invasion of Saudi troops in mid-March 2011. The Saudi repression had the full backing of the US and Britain since the island state was and is a key military base for those two powers in the geo-strategic Persian Gulf.

Similar protests were unleashed in Saudi Arabia, particularly in the oil kingdom's Eastern Province where the mainly Shia population have been historically marginalized by the hardline Sunni House of Saud. The protests in Bahrain and Saudi Arabia continue to this day. But Washington and London, along with Western media indifference, have given political cover for the ongoing repression of these protests.

In Yemen, the story is slightly different, in that the protest movement emerging in 2011 actually succeeded in ousting the US-backed regime of Ali Abdullah Saleh in 2012. Saleh was sidelined in a stitch-up deal overseen by the US and the Saudis to be replaced by his deputy, Abdrabbuh Mansour Hadi. The latter was prescribed as a "transition president" but ended up delaying the handover of democratic power that the Yemeni people had demanded in 2011. No doubt that was part of the cynical US plan to restore the old order. However, the Houthi rebels grew tired of the charade and ousted the lingering Hadi by force of arms in September 2014. The US-backed Saudi war on Yemen that started in March 2015 has ever since been aimed at repressing the Yemeni uprising in order to restore their puppet Hadi.

Regime Change

Libya and Syria represent a very different category of reaction—namely, an opportunistic regime change carried out by Washington, its European NATO allies and regional client regimes. In mid-March 2011, the US, Britain and France exploited a UN Security Council resolution under the pretext of "protecting human rights" to launch a seven-month aerial bombing campaign on Libya. That war crime resulted in the overthrow of Muammar Gaddafi and his murder at the hands of NATO-backed jihadists. Gaddafi had always been an object for Western imperialist hostility. Under the cover of Arab Spring popular revolts, the US and its allies got their chance for regime change in Libya. But seven years on, the regime change has proven to be disastrous for the people of Libya, turning the once socially developed country into a failed state of jihadist-warlord chaos. Cruel poetic justice is that Libya has haunted Europe ever since with a migration crisis owing to NATO's criminal sabotage of that country and turning the failed state into a gateway for millions of migrants from the African continent.

In Syria, minor protests in mid-March 2011 were hijacked by US and European-backed provocateurs similar to Libya, which then turned into a full-blown war. As many as 500,000 people were killed in the nearly seven-year war that was waged by the US, Britain, France, Saudi Arabia, Qatar, Israel and Turkey sponsoring jihadist mercenaries, who gravitated to Syria from dozens of countries around the world. The US-led regime-change plot to oust President Bashar Al-Assad failed mainly because Russia, Iran and Lebanon's Hezbollah intervened with military support for the Syrian state.

However, the announcement this past week by US Secretary of State Rex Tillerson that American military forces are to expand their presence in Syria shows clearly that Washington's audacious and criminal regime-change agenda persists.

Conclusion

The Arab Spring events in early 2011 were momentous. But seven years on, the progressive promise of the uprisings has yet to materialize. The recurrence of social protests in Tunisia this week is testament to the unfulfilled promise of democratic liberation for the mass of working people in that country and the wider region. The US and Europe had, and continue to have, a vested interest in maintaining the anti-democratic status quo in most of the region. The custodians of international capital managed to stymie revolution by a combination of restoration and repression. In Libya and Syria, the Western powers used the cover of the Arab Spring for opportunistic regime change with horrendous consequences.

Seven years on, the Arab Spring may seem to have been buried as a genuine popular revolutionary movement. But wherever the mass of people are oppressed by an oligarchic elite, hope for liberation will always spring eternal and is always a potential threat to the oppressors.

The Western powers may have partially succeeded in "managing" the Arab Spring. But the potential for revolt against the Western-backed capitalist order has not gone away. That potential is always there, even for an American or European Spring.

> *"Protests seem to change minds and shift public opinion. And that's why, for many, it makes sense to slander the movements they dislike."*

The Success of Protests Is Why Opponents Disparage Them

Rosemary Westwood

In the following viewpoint, Rosemary Westwood focuses on protests in the United States. She points out that the right to protest is generally acknowledged in the US, but people tend to support protests only when they agree with the cause. Otherwise, they're more likely to disparage the protesters. This is, Westwood points out, likely because protests actually do influence public opinion. Rosemary Westwood is a New Orleans–based public radio reporter and freelance writer.

As you read, consider the following questions:

1. How has the right's attitudes about protests changed over the years, according to the viewpoint?
2. What examples of protests that changed public opinion does the author provide?
3. Why does the author say that disparaging protest movements should bother people all across the political spectrum?

"Protests Change Minds and Shift Public Opinion. That's Why Opponents Are Quick to Disparage Them," by Rosemary Westwood, CBC/Radio-Canada, March 6, 2017. Reprinted by permission.

W hile the first month-and-a-half of Donald Trump's presidency has been a flurry of unpredictable antics and executive orders, one constant has emerged: that of unrelenting protests.

The dynamic dominated from inauguration day—mere sour grapes, according to Trump's fans. On that day, down in Washington, I witnessed one elderly Trump supporter yell, "Too late snowflake, you lost!" over her shoulder as she passed anti-Trump marchers. Others shrugged off protesters as jobless college graduates, and poorly dressed.

In this dismissal of protesters, Trump voters are fairly typical. It's polite, politically, to acknowledge the right to protest in a democracy, but that doesn't necessarily translate into real support.

AMERICANS ARE STILL DIVIDED OVER THE VIETNAM WAR

The Vietnam War had far-reaching consequences for the United States. It led Congress to replace the military draft with an all-volunteer force and the country to reduce the voting age to 18. It also inspired Congress to attack the "imperial" presidency through the War Powers Act, restricting a president's ability to send American forces into combat without explicit Congressional approval. Meanwhile, hundreds of thousands of Vietnamese refugees have helped restore blighted urban neighborhoods.

The Vietnam War severely damaged the U.S. economy. Unwilling to raise taxes to pay for the war, President Johnson unleashed a cycle of inflation.

The war also weakened U.S. military morale and undermined, for a time, the U.S. commitment to internationalism. The public was convinced that the Pentagon had inflated enemy casualty figures, disguising the fact that the country was engaged in a military stalemate. During the 1970s and 1980s, the United States was wary of getting involved anywhere else in the world out of fear of another Vietnam. Since then, the public's aversion to casualties inspired strict guidelines for the commitment of forces abroad and a heavy reliance on air power to project American military power.

How we feel about protests, and their legitimacy, is often self-serving.

It certainly has been for Trump's team. It threw big muscle behind the March for Life in late January, with Vice President Mike Pence and Trump advisor Kellyanne Conway making precedent-setting appearances (in the past, White House staff—including President George W. Bush—have phoned into the event, but not physically taken part). That type of protest was fine, according to team Trump.

But the protest a few days earlier—that of the Women's March on Washington, and similar marches around the world—was not. "Was under the impression that we just had an election!" Trump

The war in Vietnam deeply split the Democratic Party. As late as 1964, over 60 percent of those surveyed identified themselves in opinion polls as Democrats. The party had won seven of the previous nine presidential elections. But the prosecution of the war alienated many blue-collar Democrats, many of whom became political independents or Republicans. To be sure, other issues—such as urban riots, affirmative action, and inflation—also weakened the Democratic Party. Many former party supporters viewed the party as dominated by its anti-war faction, weak in the area of foreign policy, and uncertain about America's proper role in the world.

Equally important, the war undermined liberal reform and made many Americans deeply suspicious of government. President Johnson's Great Society programs competed with the war for scarce resources, and constituencies who might have supported liberal social programs turned against the president as a result of the war. The war also made Americans, especially the baby boomer generation, more cynical and less trusting of government and of authority.

Today, decades after the war ended, the American people remain deeply divided over the conflict's meaning. A Gallup Poll found that 53 percent of those surveyed believe that the war was "a well intentioned mistake," while 43 percent believe it was "fundamentally wrong and immoral."

"The War's Consequences," Digital History.

tweeted, while Conway remarked that she "didn't see the point" of the march, calling it needlessly divisive.

The American right didn't always see protests as futile. Back in 2009, when the Tea Party movement was shaking up the Republican party, Fox News portrayed the protests as crucial and important, and star personality Sean Hannity even fundraised for the political movement.

But the cheerleading for political dissent ended in January, after then-president Barack Obama encouraged concerned Americans to speak out about the issues raised during the campaign that were concerning them. Hannity responded by accusing Obama of stoking "out-of-control behaviour" from "anti-democratic, alt-radical" protesters.

The same hypocrisy happens in Canada, too: in January, the Rebel's Ezra Levant labelled protesters against Trump's travel ban "white leftist global extremists," just a month after he hosted his very own political protest—sorry, "rally"—against carbon taxes in Alberta. What were protesters there called? Virtuous demonstrators for freedom?

The fact is, protests seem to change minds and shift public opinion. And that's why, for many, it makes sense to slander the movements they dislike.

A striking example of the power of protest is that of the Black Lives Matter movement in the U.S., the existence of which has been correlated with a dramatic shift in American perceptions of systemic racism. In 2015, 59 per cent of Americans polled by the Pew Research Centre said they think the country needs to do more to bring equal rights to white and black Americans—up from 49 per cent only a year earlier. That's not definitive proof, but it would be hard to deny the impact of protests—such as that over the death of Freddie Gray, who died in police custody in April 2015—has had on public awareness of race issues in the U.S.

We've seen the same trends in Canada over perceptions of Indigenous issues. In 2013, a majority of Canadians didn't support Idle No More protests and believed Indigenous Canadians were the authors of their own suffering. By 2016—after years of demonstrations, coupled with the tabling of the widely publicized Truth and Reconciliation report—those views began to shift, and an Environics Institute poll found one quarter of Canadians said their views of Indigenous peoples had improved.

Although we can't prove causation in these cases, it's clear the believed power of protest is strong enough to put many people in power on guard. Indeed, with Republicans now controlling the White House, the Senate and the House, "protest" has become somewhat of a four-letter word in Washington. And Team Trump isn't stopping at simply disparaging demonstrations: it's trying to undermine their legitimacy by suggesting they are being set up by wealthy Democrats.

"It's not organic uprisings that we've seen through the last several decades," White House press secretary Sean Spicer told Fox and Friends on Feb. 6. "This has become a very paid, astro-turf type movement."

That unproven but popular claim on the right was repeated by Trump himself on Twitter a few days earlier and is considered truth by 48 per cent of Trump voters (who believe George Soros is the bankroller), according to a survey by Public Policy Polling.

It's particularly ironic, in the era of right-wing hand-wringing over free speech, that so many on the right are now quick to discount protesters. Perhaps many worry that the anti-Trump movement—thus far a virile one—will in fact sway public opinion against Republicans. But there's a destination at the end of this anti-protest trend, and it's nowhere near the realm of a healthy democracy. That should bother everyone, on both ends of the political spectrum.

> "Long-term change won't happen
> solely through protest and with only
> half the audience in the room."

The Protest Movement Is Failing

Deborah Doane

In the following viewpoint, Deborah Doane argues that protests are not effective, as evidenced by how often battles have to be fought and re-fought. The reason change isn't lasting, the author contends, is that small gains aren't accompanied by "a long-term shift in values." In order to achieve that, protesters must change their approach, and simply protesting is not enough. Deborah Doane has worked as a leader of campaigns for human rights, environmental, and economic justice issues for over 20 years and writes about international development and civil society issues.

As you read, consider the following questions:

1. What does the author mean by the term "a thin yes"?
2. Why is system change more difficult than getting particular legislative or policy changes, according to the viewpoint?
3. Why are protests that are based on anger and confrontation less likely to lead to long-term change?

Does campaigning work? I'm often asked this question. In 2010, when I was director of the World Development Movement, I was interviewed by the *Ecologist* magazine and was optimistic about the rise of activism and the opportunities to build solidarity under a Tory government. But I'm increasingly convinced that either we've been using the wrong methods in our campaigns, or we're missing something altogether.

The evidence? Environmental groups fighting U-turns on hard fought policies, like renewable energy; garment factory workers still facing working conditions that were highlighted two decades earlier; strong anti-World Trade Organisation campaigns, but yet another unjust free-trade policy, the Transatlantic Trade Partnership, looming on the horizon. We win a few campaigns, some of which I'm proud to have been involved with, but the overall direction of travel remains the same.

There are three key reasons why campaigning is failing:

1. "The Thin Yes"

Many of the so-called wins in recent years have failed because they haven't been coupled with a long-term shift in values. In the mid-90s, Shell's sinking of the *Brent Spar* was seen as a transformative event in the life of the company, a shift away from doing harm, to being a responsible corporate citizen. Today, Shell is drilling for oil in the arctic. The company didn't embed values to move away from fossil fuels, and so reverted to type. Rosie Walford, a sustainability leadership coach, refers to this as a "thin yes." It's a yes without meaning, without belief.

Micha White, one of the founders of the Occupy Movement, has also expressed his doubts. In a recent interview, he said: "Occupy was a perfect example of a social movement that should have worked according to the dominant theories of protest and activism. And yet, it failed." Instead, he thinks we need to address the issue of belief. "What I am proposing is a type of activism that focuses on creating a mental shift in people. Basically an epiphany."

2. Campaigning Can't Tackle a System

I know from experience that successful campaigns need a perfectly clear ask, ie change x law. But often what we need are large-scale systemic changes, not a simple change in the law. When I campaigned to end speculation in food commodities, I knew full well that the legal changes we sought weren't going to solve the problems in our global food system; speculators were just one piece of a very complex puzzle.

But complexity doesn't lend itself to campaigns, though some have tried. During the Copenhagen climate talks, activists used the slogan: "systems change, not climate change." But system change comes from the bottom up, it requires a whole system to engage—not just campaigners on their own—and it takes a lot of time. It doesn't inspire people to get involved, nor does it help those who need to change understand the problem.

Campaigners aren't necessarily to blame for this. Companies must understand what campaigners are asking for; governments won't listen unless there's at least many thousands of people who have signed something; and even funders are guilty of seeking short-term focused wins over providing core funding to organisations working for the longer-term.

3. Combat v. Collaboration

As campaigners, we often know the buttons to press to get short-term wins. Usually this involves anger, using words such as "stop" this or "save" that. We put up pictures of an "evil" politician or "evil" corporate bosses and expect to inspire change. Even I, a seasoned campaigner, turn off. Of course, when there's a clear corporate wrong, like Unilever's mercury poisoning in south India, an angry aggressive campaign makes sense.

But imagine, for a moment, what it feels like when someone argues with you. Your tendency is to be defensive, or to think "piss off." It's not often that someone wants to engage in a progressive change agenda while staring down the barrel of a gun.

Campaigners need to find ways to engage, either directly or indirectly, while maintaining their values. This isn't to be confused with the empty stakeholder dialogues of recent years. But long-term change won't happen solely through protest and with only half the audience in the room. This applies to both sides. Can business, for example, let activists in the room without manipulating them? Are they prepared to listen?

I don't think campaigns should cease. They open doors, they can get people thinking. But unless campaigning is coupled with approaches that are deeper, then we'll be keep fighting the same old battles until we're piling up sandbags to hold back the floods, and then it will be too late to do anything about it.

> "Society must become better at
> protesting. We must learn from
> previous protest movements'
> successes and failures, from their
> tactics and methods and from their
> determination to be inclusive."

Protests Need to Be Professionalized to Be Successful

Leah de Haan, Hugo Santiago Barrail, Ella Burdett, Mateusz Ciasnocha, Clinton Dangote, Ashiru Ayuba Dannomau, Salome Nzuki, Zakaria Ouadah, Barima Peprah-Agyemang, Laura Sanzarello, and Paula Stuurman

The question that unites the viewpoints in this chapter is "Do protests work?" But perhaps a more practical question is "What makes a protest successful?" In the following viewpoint, the authors discuss the value and importance of protest, then outline ten crucial components to successful protests. The authors are all members of the Common Futures Conversations community, an initiative aiming to create a community of young African and European community leaders and involve them in major policy discussions.

"What Makes a Successful Protest?" by Leah de Haan, Hugo Santiago Barrail, Ella Burdett, Mateusz Ciasnocha, Clinton Dangote, Ashiru Ayuba Dannomau, Salome Nzuki, Zakaria Ouadah, Barima Peprah-Agyemang, Laura Sanzarello, and Paula Stuurman, The Royal Institute of International Affairs, Chatham House, December 15, 2020. Reprinted by permission.

As you read, consider the following questions:

1. Why do the authors argue that protests ignited by specific events can be less effective than more long-term actions?
2. Why should protests be professionalized, according to this viewpoint?
3. What are the different suggestions given regarding communication?

The year of lockdowns was simultaneously a year of protest and citizen action. Throughout 2020 numerous hashtags on social media demanded our attention towards protest movements, accompanied by sometimes inspiring and sometimes horrifying images. #EndSARS, #BlackLivesMatter, #ShutItAllDown, #zwartepietisracism, #NotMyPresident, the list goes on; all demonstrating to us the commitment and fearlessness of ordinary citizens across the world asking for equal treatment and concern.

For the Common Futures Conversations community, where young people from Africa and Europe discuss key international issues, the impact of protests and citizen action also became a central focus; not least as young people were frequently found at the heart of these movements.

Many of the protest movements we have seen this year were catalysed by single events: moments that ignited long-held grievances and concerns. The most internationally recognizable is the murder of George Floyd in the United States, but there are many more examples of deaths or serious abuses that created a spark. While such sparks instigate sudden and intense swells of support, it can sometimes also mean that the resulting protests are disorganized, repeat previous mistakes and communicate their demands poorly.

Protesters are often painted as disruptors, terrorists and a nuisance, yet across the world demonstrations and direct action have been a vital form of political engagement: providing women the right to vote, people of colour the right to citizenship and people everywhere the right to stand up against populism.

In the face of crisis, panic and retrenchment in 2020, many protests found their voices demanding the change needed for marginalized groups to survive. Beyond the call for us to find our humanity, these examples demonstrate that protests are still and perhaps increasingly a method of crucial political participation.

This also means that society must become better at protesting. We must learn from previous protest movements' successes and failures, from their tactics and methods and from their determination to be inclusive.

Protest should always be seen as a legitimate avenue towards policy change and influence, and one that must therefore professionalize to make politics more reflective of societies' wants, needs and demands. To this end, ten members of the Common Futures Conversations community discuss impactful protest below.

1. Dialogue Must Be Your First Priority

Hugo Santiago Barrail (Spain)

You must focus on facilitating and strengthening dialogue mechanisms between the government and citizens. Antagonistic and violent strategies often prove counter-productive in bringing about sustainable and concrete change. Instead, protesters need to reach out both to those in power and unconvinced citizens through peaceful methods. There are many dialogue options available, including citizens' assemblies, referendums and improving the participation of civil society in policy-making.

When protests erupted in Chile in October 2019 over a rise in public transport fees, they were initially disjointed and disorganized. Many different groups, each voicing their own grievances, took to the streets and the government responded brutally. Key civil society groups and political parties then stepped in and soon enough found consensus around a single set of demands, to be pursued through a referendum process. Through the referendum, all Chileans were able to quantify support for concrete change, as a constitutional process was backed by an overwhelming majority of the electorate.

The road to achieve sustainable change is always long for protesters but through dialogue mechanisms, you can institutionalize channels to voice grievances to those in power and increase the likelihood of success.

2. Clearly Communicate What You Want

Salome Nthenya Nzuki (Kenya)

For a protest to be powerful, you must communicate clearly about why you are protesting and what changes you desire. When it comes to communication, there are clear lessons to draw from the #MyDressMyChoice protests in Kenya. In 2014, a woman in Kenya was publicly stripped by men at a bus station and groped for wearing a mini skirt. The men claimed she tempted them. Thousands of Kenyan women were angered by the act and the constant abuse of women while in transit. The incidence gave birth to the #MyDressMyChoice protests where Kenyan women took to the streets to demand the elimination of all forms of violence against women and, in particular, calling for prosecution of the men who stripped the woman and for this to be explicitly made illegal.

The protests caught the attention of women's rights organizations, the judiciary, the deputy president and the president himself. The men were arrested and prosecuted and it is now illegal in Kenya to strip a woman. Although we have a long way to go in terms of protecting women in public spaces in Kenya, the #MyDressMyChoice protests made it clear that if you assault a woman you will be prosecuted. A key reason for the success of the protest was that Kenyan women were very clear in their demands.

3. Include Digital Means of Protest Participation

Laura Sanzarello (Italy)

You should recognize the crucial role of social media's facilitation of digital protest participation. From the Arab Revolution to the #MeToo movement, both traditional and digital platforms have provided a valuable contribution through their ability to spread news, create visual representations of events and extending the potential for active engagement beyond physical barriers.

During the pandemic, mass gatherings represented a health hazard for both individuals and the wider community. However, movements like #BlackLivesMatter have nonetheless been able to obtain worldwide visibility and support. The use of hashtags, amatorial reporting, live-streaming and instant communication has enabled international engagement, reduced the chances of suppression and manipulation of stories and shown the importance of digital protest participation.

Digital participation's effectiveness does not just apply to individual action, it can also help draw the attention of international actors. This can pressure governments to engage with the matters animating protesters, demonstrating that both in-person and virtual contributions can help encourage impactful resolutions.

4. Listen to Everyone's Concerns
Clinton Dangote (Cameroon)

You will need a broad coalition of many different people to support your protest if you want it to create change. Often protests occur when governmental policies are inconsistent with the needs of citizens. This can lead to urgent calls for change and one way to bring about this change is in the form of protests. However, it is crucial that protest movements do not make the same mistakes as governments. They must amplify the voices of the marginalized and the disenfranchised. This involves making sure to include a wide range of voices and not just listening to concerns and solutions of the first people to join a protest.

A protest can only bring about valuable policy change when it is well-planned, focused, and the demands are clear. Protesters must express their displeasure and constructively present their demands as one voice. Proactive leaders must engage all protesters in a dialogue and find common demands to meet their needs. This way a protest can mirror the way the general public feels about a given policy.

5. Use Social Media, Where One Click Makes a Difference

Mateusz Ciasnocha (Poland)

You should leverage social media for the benefits of protests. Social media has changed and is continuously changing our lives. During the earthquakes in Nepal or the terrorist attacks in Christchurch and Paris, our friends were able to mark themselves as "safe." These small actions created a unique sense of global unity, which we should build on when it comes to protests. Creating a campaign, a new group, or even proposing a new overlay for your profile photo are all happening today. These campaigns can go viral and are a great mechanism for creating momentum for your demands for change.

It is clear that our actions on social media can lead to positive change. Protest movements should take the time to create frameworks and mechanisms, to help transform momentum into real positive change in an inclusive, transparent and efficient manner.

6. Create Inclusive Working Groups

Barima Peprah-Agyemang (Ghana)

You should create frameworks for protest participants that work together to approach problems and create inclusive solutions. Protest movements are often dismissed by governments by deploying excuses along the lines of "their demands are unclear" or "they have no solutions," as happened with the Occupy Wall Street protests. A way to ensure that protest movements are able to stand together in support of solutions is by forming "working groups." These groups gather the concerns of the protesters, sit down to analyse the responses and then develop specific demands and solutions that represent what protesters want.

This requires professionalizing a protest movement and will create a reliance on people from professions like law, community organizing and economics, but should be open for any protestor to join. This would enable protest movements to capture varying opinions that enrich the specific solutions being prepared.

The work of these groups would not only pre-empt standard excuses used by governments to avoid change, but would also enable them to project an image of seriousness to the world, an ingredient necessary to secure support for the struggle.

7. Professionalize Your Media Outreach

Paula Stuurman (Netherlands)

You need to professionalize your approach to communicating the protest internationally. Real-time news reporting pushes events to the forefront at lightning speed but replaces them just as quickly. In 2020 the world saw many protests met with violence, for example when US militias policed the streets as a response to Black Lives Matter protests or when police conducted violent acts against protestors in Belarus. We saw these events because protestors themselves provided videos of the violence, but they then quickly disappeared from the world stage of media attention.

Through meticulously documenting protests, altercations and human rights violations—harnessing the power of social media to continue to inform a global audience—protestors can inspire public outrage, support and ultimately policy changes once their voice can no longer be ignored.

To maintain the media's attention and overcome the 24-hour news-cycle, protestors need to develop a professional approach to documenting protests to magnify their voices internationally. This reporting must be honest and unbiased, drawing on the lessons from human rights organisations' techniques to maintain the public's attention.

8. Connect with Social Activists from Across the World

Zakaria Ouadah (Algeria)

You must engage with social activists in other countries who are also striving for change. Today's technological resources demonstrate how effective virtual spaces are for connecting and working together, something that the Common Futures Conversations platform has demonstrated to me. Engaging with international networks composed of social activists who can support your movements and provide you a space to share your experiences can be very advantageous to your cause.

It is crucial to link up with organizations in your own country that are working towards similar goals, but do not underestimate the value of connecting to other social activists as well.

The networking, support and expanded skills resulting from engaging with others can help protest movements put themselves into a position where the authorities are forced to enter a phase of dialogue and hopefully answer the demands given to them.

9. Citizen Action Should Start in Schools

Ella Burdett (United Kingdom)

You should make sure to include young people in discussions on citizen action and educate them on protests, policy change and political engagement. From an early age, people should learn that their voice is important and how they personally can impact politics and policy. The issue is, however, that schools do not sufficiently educate children on how policy works and in failing to do so send them out into the world without the tools to change it.

In the United Kingdom there are Personal, Social, Health and Economic (PSHE) lessons, but neither the statutory nor the optional subjects include political participation, policy change or citizen action. Yet, as participation is integral to democracy, education on civic and political engagement is essential for creating citizens who understand how to critically participate in a democratic society.

Compulsory civics classes in secondary schools would therefore provide all children with equal tools to make their voice heard. In the absence of this, take any opportunity to educate younger people in your society on the importance of standing up for your principles and the mechanisms available to succeed.

10. Combine All Non-Violent Protest Mechanisms

Ashiru Ayuba Dannomau (Nigeria)

You should learn from previous successful protests and research all the non-violent approaches that could be effective. There are many ways that non-violent protest approaches are effective; they convey a vital message to both government officials and citizens that peoples' lives matter. In this way, drawing on lessons from previous non-violent approaches helps protect the life of every individual and allows for strategic tactics to pursue the change you wish to see.

Protest organizers must learn about past methods that have worked, why they may be effective and relevant to your context, and then ensure the whole movement learns these lessons collectively. It will also help protest leaders be more strategic in their tactics, in their approach to governments and when moulding the ideas of citizens into policy demands.

During the #EndSARS protests in Nigeria, I witnessed how people lost their lives and property because they came out to protest against police brutality. I also saw how this youth movement repeated past mistakes because everyone was saying different things and there was a lack of coordination in message and action.

We must learn from previous protest movements to prevent such confusion, all the while keeping in mind that whenever someone is killed, injured or has their property destroyed during a protest that it is hazardous to your community.

*"Protests played a large
role in mobilizing the
Democratic party during the
2018 congressional elections."*

Protest Can Motivate and Organize the Political Party That Is Out of Power

Matt Grossmann

In the following viewpoint, an excerpted podcast interview, Matt Grossmann discusses the power of protest to change political parties and election outcomes with political scientist Michael Heaney. The Trump era spawned a strong wave of protests and demonstrations, allowing researchers to study the power of protest in the modern age. Matt Grossmann is director of the Institute for Public Policy and Social Research and professor of political science at Michigan State University. He is host of the Political Research Digest *at Niskanen Center.*

As you read, consider the following questions:

1. Why does Heaney call the Trump presidency "exceptional" in terms of his studies?
2. According to the viewpoint, how did resistance protests help Democrats in the 2018 election?
3. What does Heaney predict for the future of protest in America?

Matt Grossmann: This week on the Science of Politics, how protests move parties and elections. For the Niskanen Center, I'm Matt Grossmann. Protests are heating up over police brutality and COVID-19 lockdowns in the middle of a presidential election year. How much do protests respond to the political moment? And can they change election outcomes? New research suggests that protests can change partisanship and voting, helping liberal and conservative protesters leave their mark. And the Trump protest era has been quite active.

Today, I talked to Michael Heaney of the University of Glasgow and the University of Michigan about his research on protest under the Trump administration. He finds that protests will respond to the party of the president and can help the party out of power organize and voice its concerns. He also coauthored a recent review, "The Science of Contemporary Street Protests." The new review looks at the new era of protests, finding a big increase under Trump.

Michael Heaney: This article was coauthored with Dana Fisher, Kenneth Andrews, Neil Karen, Erica Chenoweth, Tommy Leon, Nathan Perkins, and Jeremy Pressman. And this talks about what we've learned about protests both by using event counting methods and by looking at surveys of people participating in protests. And many people traditionally think about the 1960s as the pinnacle of protest in the United States. And there's a lot to be said for that perspective, but we think it's also important to recognize that there's a new era of broad mass protest, which began in the United States roughly in the late 1990s with the global justice movement.

And of course the internet played a huge role in supporting these new protests. But even considering the rising prominence of protest since the late 1990s, the period of the Trump presidency stands out as exceptional. So in this article we really looked at this recent period. We've noted that the Trump era has witnessed some of the largest protests that we've ever seen in American history, especially the Women's March in 2017. We've seen coordinated protests across the United States and worldwide, but we've also seen an amazing diversity of topics from the Women's March, support for science, anti-gun violence, racial justice, protests for white supremacy, the right to life protest, pro-Trump protests, et cetera. So there's been a cornucopia of different kinds of protests during the Trump era. There's also been a continuing evolution of the ways that people protest. Of course, we've seen traditional protest marches and demonstrations, but we've also seen new ways of doing online protests and even in-person protests, such as car caravans.

We've learned that protesters are widely motivated by their belief about whether their voices are being heard through other channels. That's a big part of the reason why protests grow after people perceive there to be an unjust or adverse electoral outcome. And then the protest tends to diminish as other opportunities for raising their voice present themselves. We see protests coming both from the left and the right sides of the political spectrum, but these protesters in these two different groups are differently motivated. So during the Trump era, right-leaning protesters have been more likely than left protestors to see the American political system as effective and solving problems and just see elections as creating responsive government. Left-leaning protesters are more likely to embrace a role for third parties in American politics, and to acknowledge the potential effectiveness of incivility and violence during protest.

[...]

Matt Grossmann: Heaney's work builds on his prior research on how partisanship motivates protests.

Michael Heaney: Well, my prior protest-oriented research focused on the antiwar movement in the United States. Although I also look somewhat at the Tea Party and Occupy Wall Street movements, I was also interested in how, and the extent to which activists identities are tied to political parties. Most notably this work culminated as a book with Fabio Rojas titled *Party in the Street*, and that was published by Cambridge University press in 2015.

As protest moves into the Trump era. I wanted to expand upon this agenda in two ways. First, I wanted to look at a broader range of issues. Luckily, the Trump presidency has brought out opposition on so many topics. That's been good for research. That's helped to make my research broader in scope. And second, I wanted to look at activist identities as motivated by factors other than just partisanship. I've also been exploring issue identities and ideological identities.

Matt Grossmann: He says the Trump protests are not all part of one resistance.

Michael Heaney: I think that the conventional wisdom on the Trump resistance protests that is broadly correct, is that these protests have brought a new generation of activists into the streets. This is particularly true for women and feminists. Indeed, the Women's March has had a big impact on the political mobilization of the left. I think that the conventional wisdom is also correct that these resistance protests have helped to introduce people to electoral institutional politics, organizations such as Indivisible played a vital role on this point.

Where I think the conventional wisdom is misguided, it has to do with seeing all of these left leaning protests as linked to the Resistance with a capital R, that we might think of as being fundamentally responsive to Trump. Many protests are actually outside the resistance.

For example, the global climate strike and protest against school shootings are not really resistance that is anti-Trump motivated, as much as they are issue motivated or linked to longer standing social movements.

Matt Grossmann: He finds differences across even liberal protests by candidate and type.

Michael Heaney: The most recent surveys that I conducted were in January 2020 at the Women's March, and then No War on Iran protests. I fielded surveys in Los Angeles, New York and Washington, DC. I didn't find big differences between people in different cities, however I did find big differences between the Women's March and the No War on Iran protests.

Women's marches were significantly more likely to think of themselves as part of the resistance. The antiwar protesters were more neutral on this label. Women's Marches were significantly more likely to place themselves on the left side of the moderate middle of the political spectrum. Whereas antiwar protesters were more likely to place themselves on the far left, radical side of the political.

Also women's marches were significantly more likely to throw their support behind Elizabeth Warren. Antiwar protesters were more enamored with Bernie Sanders. There weren't very many people in either group that were particularly excited about Joe Biden, and of course, everyone disliked Donald Trump.

Matt Grossmann: These interviews were recorded before the latest round of black led mass protests against police brutality in the wake of the killing of George Floyd. But Heaney … had already been thinking about the racial dynamics of protest. Heaney says black activists tend to focus on minority focused actions.

Michael Heaney: So actually I'm looking at this question in a current project with Fabio Rojas, and Mona Adem of Indiana University. What we find is that African American activists, and activists in other minority racial and ethnic groups, tend to avoid these large white dominated protest events because they don't focus on the issues that these activists are most concerned with.

For example, African American activists care about gender based inequalities, but they tend to be focused more on issues such as police violence against people of color. When African American and other minority activists do participate in white dominated movements, they tend to see themselves as allies rather than core participants to the movement. African American and other minority activists have also channeled their activism into other kinds of topics.

For example, they've been more focused on responding to killings of persons of color, through locally-based protests rather than large national gatherings. They've also made creative use of online activists. For example, a recent book by Sarah Jackson, Moya Bailey and Brooke Wells called *Hashtag Activism* details many of these online activist efforts. It shows how efforts such as Ferguson and Trayvon Martin become a means of coordinating online activist community. Part of the reason that we don't see these activists at large protests, it's not because they're not involved in activism, but they're using other kinds of tasks.

[...]

Matt Grossmann: And Heaney finds that resistance protests helped Democrats and the 2018 election.

Michael Heaney: Protests played a large role in mobilizing the Democratic party during the 2018 congressional elections. Most notably the Women's March, Indivisible and Move On helped this process along. Statistical evidence shows that there was a significant positive association between congressional candidates participating in the Women's March and their winning in the Democratic primary and the general election in 2018. My recent surveys show less of a connection between social movements and electoral success in the Democratic presidential primary. Perhaps the issue there is that activists were split in their support for Elizabeth Warren and Bernie Sanders.

[...]

Matt Grossmann: Heaney says [the latest antilockdown conservative protests have] been very unusual.

Michael Heaney: We don't like the way things are going with COVID. It's not realistic for everyone to go to Washington DC and protest about it. They've also flipped the preference for demonstrations on their head. So now we see conservatives preferring demonstrations more than liberals, but it's usually the other way around. Now a big difference from the Tea Party protest during the Obama era is that they've been focused on lower levels of governments, governors, and concentrating on the states rather than the federal government. It's also been very unusual that the president of the United States is encouraging opposition to some of his own policy.

Matt Grossmann: Other protestors may be fearing mass mobilization, but Heaney says they can strategically change tactics even toward electoral politics.

Michael Heaney: Protest is one manifestation of activism, but activists have other tools in their toolkit, such as online activism and electoral participation. Protest is a go to tactic when people feel that their voices are not being heard through other channels, but if these other tactics are working, activists shift their energies there. So I think that the success of Democrats in the 2018 congressional election has suggested to many activists that it's within their grasp to vote Trump out. At the same time, there have been other significant protest since 2018, most importantly, the 2019 Global Climate Strike reflects this growing strength of the international climate movement. And then of course, there's also been protests related to COVID-19.

[…]

Matt Grossmann: Heaney says polarization means protests are here to stay. Whoever wins this November.

Michael Heaney: I think that we're going to see protest as being an important element of American politics, regardless of who the next President is. If Trump wins reelection, we'll see another round of massive protests. Likewise, if Biden becomes President, I think we'll see another round of Tea Party style protests.

Given polarization, people don't feel like their voices are being heard through their traditional methods of participation. So I think we're going to see people turning out and quite unhappy, no matter what the outcome is.

Matt Grossmann: The next step for Heaney is looking at the Trump protests electoral impact.

Michael Heaney: The next thing that I'm doing is writing a book called *American Democracy Under Protest*. And the goal is to understand protest as a fundamental tool of democratic participation. Most of the research that has been done in the past has really looked at protest as something that's separate from the fundamental democratic processes like voting.

But I think that these two things are closely connected. And I want to look at that more systematically and to do that, I'm looking at protests that have taken place since Trump has been elected, as well as the relationship with electoral participation, such as how the Women's March has helped encourage democratic victories and also looking at things like the way that people are participating through social media.

[…]

Michael Heaney: Sociologists have been a lot more interested in protests at least within the United States, than political scientists have. Protests for sociologists has been a central and interesting political phenomenon that they've wanted to understand who participated and why they participated and how they participated, how this manifested other people's grievances.

And also, I think part of what has made sociologists interested in this is that they've seen protesters as being outside the political system. And sociology as a discipline is very interested in understanding outsiders. Whereas political science has a strong focus on institutions. And so that's why there's a strong interest in, for example, why people vote and who they vote for. And political scientists, at least in the United States, has been less interested in these kind of informal mechanisms of participation. And so I think that the next step for research is to try to understand better the relationship between protests and formal institutions.

So my perspective would be that when people see the formal institutions as broken, they're more likely to turn to protest as something they can do. And I think that if we can connect the study of protest to these formal institutions, that political scientists will have a greater interest in it.

[...]

Periodical and Internet Sources Bibliography

The following articles have been selected to supplement the diverse views presented in this chapter.

Maggie Astor, "Why Protest Movements Are 'Civil' Only in Retrospect," *New York Times*, June 16, 2020. https://www.nytimes.com/2020/06/16/us/politics/us-protests-history-george-floyd.html.

Erica Chenoweth, "The Future of Nonviolent Resistance," *Journal of Democracy*, July 2020. https://www.journalofdemocracy.org/articles/the-future-of-nonviolent-resistance-2/.

Dennis Gilbert, "Ending the Vietnam War, in Context," Letter to the Editor, *Eugene Weekly*, June 10, 2021. https://eugeneweekly.com/2021/06/10/ending-the-vietnam-war-in-context/.

Nathan Heller, "Is There Any Point to Protesting?" *New Yorker*, August 14, 2017. https://www.newyorker.com/magazine/2017/08/21/is-there-any-point-to-protesting.

Robert Levering, "How 1971's Mayday Actions Rattled Nixon and Kept Vietnam from Becoming a Forever War," *Waging Nonviolence*, April 29, 2021. https://wagingnonviolence.org/2021/04/spring-offensive-mayday-1971-nixon-vietnam-antiwar/.

Shom Mazumder, "What Protests Can (and Can't) Do," FiveThirtyEight, June 8, 2020. https://fivethirtyeight.com/features/what-protests-can-do/.

Phillip Morris, "To Enact Change in the World, We Must Protest," *National Geographic*, June 6, 2020. https://www.nationalgeographic.com/history/article/to-enact-change-world-we-must-protest.

David Robson, "The '3.5 Percent Rule': How a Small Minority Can Change the World," *BBC Future*, May 13, 2019. https://www.bbc.com/future/article/20190513-it-only-takes-35-of-people-to-change-the-world.

Ashley Smith, "Which Way Forward for the Anti-War Movement?" Counterpunch, June 26, 2008. https://www.counterpunch.org/2008/06/26/which-way-forward-for-the-antiwar-movement-2/.

Britany Trujillo and Robert Byrne, "A Restaurant's Role in Racial Justice," Technomic. https://www.technomic.com/newsroom /restaurants-role-racial-justice.

Heather Whipps and Brandon Specktor, "13 Significant Protests That Changed the Course of History," Live Science, June 4, 2020. https://www.livescience.com/16153-10-significant-political -protests.html.

Gilda Zwerman and Michael Schwartz, "How 'Good' Social Movements Can Triumph over 'Bad' Ones," *Scientific American*, March 16, 2021. https://www.scientificamerican.com/article /how-lsquo-good-rsquo-social-movements-can-triumph-over -lsquo-bad-rsquo-ones/.

OPPOSING
VIEWPOINTS®
SERIES

CHAPTER 2

Are Peaceful Protests More Effective Than Violent Protests?

Chapter Preface

The previous chapter addressed whether or not protest is an effective way to bring about social and policy change. In the following chapter, the viewpoints are concerned with what kind of protest is more likely to be effective.

While protest is not peaceful by definition, when the intent is violence, actions are typically not called protests but rather rebellions or terrorism or some other term more associated with violent resistance. The influence of leaders such as Martin Luther King Jr. and Mahatma Gandhi have cemented the view of social protests as nonviolent. When protests become violent, they are usually considered a failure on the part of the movement or simply a demonstration that got out of hand. However, not all protests end peacefully, and many don't start that way. Smashed windows and burning cars are not always unintended consequences but often are methods of protest.

In the viewpoints that follow, authors debate the merits and drawbacks of each kind of action. The chapter opens with a viewpoint detailing the history of violence that preceded Gandhi's nonviolent resistance to British colonial rule in India. It closes with a thoughtful discussion of what makes a peaceful protest turn violent. In between we hear from authors who argue that disruption of society is often justified and even necessary as long as it's nonviolent, from authors who say that violent protests do more harm that good to the causes they support, and excerpts from a debate about the merits of nonviolence as a strategy of the civil rights movement by leaders of that movement themselves.

> *"While it is the memory of Gandhi and non-violence that is now marked by British politicians when they visit India, the other side to the story is very real, and should not be forgotten."*

India's Resistance to British Rule Was Not Always Nonviolent

Joseph McQuade

We always think of India's struggle for independence from Britain as a peaceful, if difficult, campaign. However, in the following viewpoint, Joseph McQuade argues that the struggle was not totally nonviolent. Violent resistance to British colonial rule had broken out as early as the mid-eighteenth century. McQuade details the resistance that came before and led to Mohandas Gandhi's nonviolent rebellion. Joseph McQuade is a scholar who studies the role of terrorism and insurgency in post-colonial India and Burma.

As you read, consider the following questions:

1. What was India's "First War of Independence"?
2. How does the author describe the role of terrorism in freeing India from Britain?
3. How did Britain establish control of India in the first place?

The popular view of India's journey to independence from British rule is the famous story of Mohandas Gandhi's extraordinary campaign of non-violent protest. It is a heritage still marked today during international state visits.

But there was another, often forgotten—and much less peaceful—side to the struggle for Indian independence.

British colonial rule in India had been established through a series of wars fought across the subcontinent from the mid-18th century onwards. It was bloody and gradual, and rested on a thin foundation of coercion and military dominance.

This was made painfully clear by the uprising of 1857, in which a series of rebellions erupted across northern India, seriously undermining imperial confidence. Although the mutiny was crushed, the memory of it continued to inspire generations of Indian anti-colonialists, who would later refer to it as the First War of Independence.

While the events of 1857 were described by the colonial authorities in various terms including "mutiny," "rebellion" and "insurgency," the first act of anti-colonial violence to be given the label of "terrorism" was carried out 40 years later.

In 1897, two brothers assassinated WC Rand, a civil service officer responsible for dealing with an outbreak of bubonic plague in the city of Pune, whose measures of forced home entry, bodily examinations and segregation were considered extremely heavy-handed.

Later, after colonial officials decided to partition the prosperous province of Bengal in 1905, non-violent forms of popular protest were accompanied by the growth of secret cells of revolutionaries who sought to undermine British imperial authority using targeted assassinations and bomb attacks.

Even though the partition was annulled in 1911, the revolutionary organisations it spawned did not disappear. In fact, they expanded massively.

On November 1, 1913, Indian revolutionaries living in San Francisco published the first issue of *Ghadar*, or "Mutiny," a radical weekly newspaper that quickly developed a global readership. By the summer of 1914, the Ghadar Party they founded was an international organisation, with more than 6,000 members and networks throughout North America, Europe, and Asia.

In February 1915, revolutionaries connected to the Ghadar Party attempted to overthrow British rule through an ambitious uprising across northern India. Led by Rash Behari Bose, a veteran revolutionary who had personally attempted to assassinate the Viceroy of India in 1912, the revolutionaries tried to convince the Indian Army to mutiny by disseminating propaganda in Lahore, Rawalpindi, and Meerut.

The plot was foiled after a British-paid spy penetrated the organisation, prompting a huge crackdown in which hundreds of radicals were detained. Bose was forced to flee India, escaping to Japan where he would live out the rest of his life in exile.

The following month, Ghadar revolutionaries in the US acquired two ships, the *Annie Larsen* and the *Maverick*. They planned to land a huge arms shipment in Calcutta on Christmas Day. It was timed to coincide with another planned uprising in Burma, then still a part of British India, and a raid on the prison islands of the Andamans, in which incarcerated radicals would be liberated to take up arms against the British.

Like the February uprising, the Christmas Day plot was detected and foiled by the colonial intelligence services, which had expanded their operations to a global scale in response to the transnational reach of Ghadar.

With the implementation of strict wartime legislation such as the Defence of India Act, 1916 was a turning point for the revolutionary campaign, which was driven underground by imperial intelligence services, who detained several hundred suspected revolutionaries.

India's revolutionary organisations did not vanish after World War I. As the war measures expired, the colonial government implemented the 1919 Rowlatt Act in an effort to extend executive powers into the postwar period. The proposed legislation permitted suspects to be interned without trial and allowed political cases to be tried without juries. This provoked outrage among the majority of the Indian population, who viewed it as an insult to their loyal service during the war.

At a gathering in Amritsar in April 1919, imperial troops opened fire on a crowd of unarmed protesters, killing at least 379 people and sparking nationwide anger.

Peace in His Time

This is the context in which Mohandas Gandhi (usually called Mahatma out of respect) emerged to lead the Indian nationalist movement, which he rallied with a message of peaceful non-cooperation and non-violent resistance. Nonetheless, the more violent anti-colonial organisations formed in the years before and after World War I influenced both anti-colonial politics and imperial security right up until India's independence and partition in 1947.

After the Second World War, many British officials were unsettled by fear of the Indian National Army, a military organisation made up of Indian prisoners of war released from Japanese custody and led by the famous nationalist Subhas Chandra Bose.

Despite being defeated militarily, the INA strengthened British unease that the continued occupation of India would be met by violent resistance. Following the end of the war, the trial of INA prisoners provided a serious problem for colonial legitimacy and helped to stoke the mass nationalism that forced Britain to withdraw in 1947.

So while it is the memory of Gandhi and non-violence that is now marked by British politicians when they visit India, the other side to the story is very real, and should not be forgotten.

Recalling the history of Indian revolutionaries isn't just a matter of filling in historical gaps. It can help us gain some perspective on modern society by looking at the recent past.

And now a visit to India by the British Prime Minister Theresa May has included a pledge with the Indian PM Narendra Modi that India and the UK will work together to fight terrorism in both countries. It is not known whether or not they discussed the role that terrorism played in securing India's independence from Britain. But perhaps they should have done—they would have had plenty to talk about.

> "Throughout history, many laws and
> policies produced in democracies
> were grossly unjust. These include
> laws that institutionalised slavery ...
> or prohibited women and people of
> colour from voting."

Nonviolent Disruption Is Often Justified

Samuel Alexander

Successful protests can be peaceful, but that doesn't mean they aren't disruptive. In fact, disruption is often part of the plan. In the following viewpoint, Samuel Alexander reacts to a series of climate change demonstrations that disrupted traffic in several Australian cities. The author argues that when laws or policies are clearly unjust, then civil disobedience is justified. Samuel Alexander is a research fellow at the Sustainable Society Institute at the University of Melbourne in Melbourne, Australia.

As you read, consider the following questions:

1. What are the three demands of the Extinction Rebellion movement?
2. How does the author define "civil disobedience"?
3. When, according to the viewpoint, is civil disobedience justified?

I f you live in a major Australian city, expect your daily routine to be disrupted this week. Protest group Extinction Rebellion is carrying out a week of flash mobs, sit-ins and marches to block traffic and bring more attention to the pressing problems of climate change and biodiversity loss. Many arrests are expected.

Extinction Rebellion protesters say peaceful civil disobedience is an important social and political strategy for achieving a just and sustainable world.

Their protest actions may make us feel uncomfortable, annoyed or worse. But it is important that the general public understands the reasoning that underpins civil disobedience and why this radical strategy is being deployed this week.

Resistance Movements Are No Stranger to Law-Breaking

The Extinction Rebellion movement has three bold demands of governments. First, government should declare a climate and ecological "emergency." Second, by 2025 governments should decarbonise the economy and halt biodiversity loss. Third, citizens' assemblies should be established to work with scientists to inform environmental policy-making.

Many aspects of Extinction Rebellion deserve, and have received, critical analysis, including whether its decarbonisation timeframe is unrealistic and whether their disruption tactics will alienate rather than inspire the general public.

The movement's civil disobedience strategy is one of its most controversial. Civil disobedience is defined as public, non-violent and conscientious breaches of law that aim to change government policies.

Law-abiding citizens are right to be concerned about others deliberately breaking the law to advance their social, political or environmental goals. But many of the most significant social and political advances over the past century owe much to social movements that relied on this tactic. Think of Gandhi's independence movement against British rule in India, the suffragette fight for the right of women to vote and the US civil rights movement.

These precedents raise the question: might future societal advances also demand peaceful acts of civil disobedience?

Civil Disobedience: The Case for and Against

Imperfect though it is, the basic theory of democracy is that we vote on who represents us in government. In this way, democratic societies are said to have created the institutions and processes needed for their own peaceful improvement.

So critics of civil disobedience argue that people shouldn't just break the law because they disagree with it. They say if you do not like a policy or law, you are free to campaign for change, including for the election of a new government.

But proponents of civil disobedience argue that democracy is flawed and in some cases, non-violent breaches of law can be justified.

First, they say laws and policies can be shaped undemocratically by powerful mass media, corporate lobby groups, or billionaires. Proponents say citizens do not always owe political allegiance to laws and policies that are not produced through fair, robust, and representative democratic processes.

Second, many political and legal theorists say just because something is enshrined in law, that does not mean it is necessarily just. This was the view advanced by American writer and philosopher Henry David Thoreau in his 1849 essay *Civil Disobedience*, which inspired both Gandhi and Martin Luther King Jr.

Throughout history, many laws and policies produced in democracies were grossly unjust. These include laws that institutionalised slavery, legally entrenched racial segregation, criminalised homosexuality or particular religious practices, or prohibited women and people of colour from voting.

When a law or policy is clearly unfair, a case can be made that there is a place for civil disobedience. We must accept that even laws produced in a democracy get it wrong sometimes.

Will Extinction Rebellion Fall on the Right Side of History?

The Extinction Rebellion is promoting civil disobedience because it says across the world, governments have failed to respond adequately to the climate crisis and the steep decline in wildlife populations. It argues that the political system underpinning this failure must be resisted, even if this causes inconvenience to the general public.

The movement's supporters include 250 Australian academics who signed an open letter saying they feel a "moral duty" to rebel and "defend life itself."

It could be argued that the activists should wait until governments take action. But judging by recent history—including a lack of substantial progress at last month's UN climate summit—an adequate, timely global response to the climate crisis seems highly

THE ONLY WEAPON IS THE WEAPON OF PROTEST

We are here this evening for serious business. We are here in a general sense because first and foremost we are American citizens and we are determined to apply our citizenship to the fullness of its meaning. We are here also because of our love for democracy, because of our deep-seated belief that democracy transformed from thin paper to thick action is the greatest form of government on earth.

We are here, we are here this evening because we're tired now. And I want to say that we are not here advocating violence. We have never done that. I want it to be known throughout Montgomery and throughout this nation that we are Christian people. We believe in the Christian religion. We believe in the teachings of Jesus. The only weapon that we have in our hands this evening is the weapon of protest. That's all.

And certainly, certainly, this is the glory of America, with all of its faults. This is the glory of our democracy. If we were incarcerated behind the iron curtains of a Communistic nation we couldn't do this. If we were dropped in the dungeon of a totalitarian regime we couldn't unlikely. In this case, waiting for government action means being complicit in an unjust system.

Some people will inevitably dismiss Extinction Rebellion protesters as troublemakers and criminals. But their actions must be assessed against the big picture. The world's best climate scientists overwhelmingly agree that if global warming is not kept below the 1.5°C limit, Earth's natural and human systems will suffer dire consequences. The legitimacy of Extinction Rebellion's disobedience must be weighed against the wrongs that triggered it.

As Extinction Rebellion causes chaos in our cities, we must avoid superficial, kneejerk reactions. Whatever your views on civil disobedience, the climate emergency would be far less serious if governments had taken action decades ago. Further inaction will only lead to more numerous and active social movements, driven by the same mixture of love and rage that provoked Extinction Rebellion.

do this. But the great glory of American democracy is the right to protest for right. My friends, don't let anybody make us feel that we are to be compared in our actions with the Ku Klux Klan or with the White Citizens Council. There will be no crosses burned at any bus stops in Montgomery. There will be no white persons pulled out of their homes and taken out on some distant road and lynched for not cooperating. There will be nobody amid, among us who will stand up and defy the Constitution of this nation. We only assemble here because of our desire to see right exist. My friends, I want it to be known that we're going to work with grim and bold determination to gain justice on the buses in this city.

And we are not wrong, we are not wrong in what we are doing. If we are wrong, the Supreme Court of this nation is wrong. If we are wrong, the Constitution of the United States is wrong. If we are wrong, God Almighty is wrong. If we are wrong, Jesus of Nazareth was merely a utopian dreamer that never came down to earth. If we are wrong, justice is a lie. Love has no meaning. And we are determined here in Montgomery to work and fight until justice runs down like water, and righteousness like a mighty stream.

Montgomery Bus Boycott speech, delivered by Martin Luther King Jr. at the Holt Street Baptist Church in Montgomery, Alabama, December 5, 1955.

> "*You cannot make a moral appeal in the midst of an amoral society.*"

Nonviolence Will Not Work When the Other Side Is Willing to Kill You

Library of Congress

In the following viewpoint, an article from the Library of Congress archives, we hear from several people who were involved in the US civil rights movement in the 1950s and 1960s. Though the movement itself was largely nonviolent and the movement's leader, Martin Luther King Jr., was dedicated to nonviolence, not everyone involved was sure that this would be an effective approach. This viewpoint provides modern readers with a glimpse into the debates that went on behind the scenes of the movement.

As you read, consider the following questions:

1. Why did Chuck McDew say that nonviolence of the kind Gandhi practiced wouldn't work in the United States?
2. If civil rights protesters felt threatened, why did they commit to nonviolent actions in their protests?
3. How do the people quoted in the viewpoint justify their use of weapons to protect themselves?

"Nonviolent Philosophy and Self Defense," Library of Congress.

The success of the movement for African American civil rights across the South in the 1960s has largely been credited to activists who adopted the strategy of nonviolent protest. Leaders such as Martin Luther King, Jr., Jim Lawson, and John Lewis believed wholeheartedly in this philosophy as a way of life, and studied how it had been used successfully by Mahatma Gandhi to protest inequality in India. They tried to literally "love your enemies" and practiced pacifism in all circumstances. But other activists were reluctant to devote their lives to nonviolence, and instead saw it as simply a tactic that could be used at marches and sit-ins to gain sympathy for their cause and hopefully change the attitudes of those who physically attacked them. Many interviewees in the Civil Rights History Project discuss their own personal views of nonviolence and how they grappled with it in the face of the daily threats to their lives.

When the Student Nonviolent Coordinating Committee (SNCC) was founded at a conference for college students in 1960, members debated whether the group should adopt nonviolence as a way of life or as a tactical strategy for its mission. Courtland Cox remembers the debates at this meeting: "One of the things that the nonviolent people's philosophy—those people, they felt that, you know, you could appeal to men's hearts. You know, my view, and which I've said to them, was that you might as well appeal to their livers, because they're both organs of the body. There was nothing to that. You did not—you engaged in nonviolence because the other side had overwhelming force. There was not a sense that the other side would do the right thing if you told them, because at the end of the day, the other side knew what it was doing to you better than you did." Chuck McDew was also at this meeting and recalls, "My position was when Gandhi tried nonviolence in South Africa he was beaten, jailed, and run out of the country. As I said, in the United States nonviolence won't work. Because when Gandhi used, in India, the tactic of having people lay down on railroad tracks to protest, I said, 'and it worked.' I said, 'But if a group of black people lay down on railroad tracks here, in South Carolina, Georgia, Alabama, Mississippi, Texas, Louisiana, any of these Southern states, a train would run you over and back up to make certain you're dead. You cannot make a moral appeal in the midst of an amoral society.' And I said that it was not immoral. We lived in a society that was amoral, and as such, nonviolence was not going to work. And so, I said I couldn't and the people with me could not join Dr. King. And, uh, 'Thank you, but no thanks.'"

Even though activists used nonviolence at protests to gain sympathy for their cause, arming themselves with guns for self-protection was not uncommon. Mildred Bond Roxborough was a longtime secretary of the National Association for the Advancement of Colored People (NAACP) and traveled throughout the South regularly to help with organizing. She tells a story about driving through Mississippi with Medgar Evers during a particularly violent time: "We had had two branch presidents who had been killed just before this particular time. It was difficult to believe that these people would continue to carry on like this because the situation was so oppressive in Mississippi. We were driving one night and I had taken off my shoes and felt something on the floor which was cold. I said to Medgar, 'What is this? Maybe I can move it.' He said, 'Well, that's my shotgun you have your feet on.' Of course my feet flew up. But this is just to give you an idea of the sense of the environment."

The Deacons for Defense and Justice was a group founded in Jonesboro, Louisiana, in 1964 to organize men to guard the homes of activists and to protect them while they traveled. A second branch was started in Bogalusa, Louisiana, the following year. The Hicks family was protected by the Deacons, and Barbara Collins, the daughter of activist Robert Hicks, reflects on her father's position on armed self-defense in an interview with the family: "And my dad always said, 'What kind of man—?' You know, Martin Luther King was a good man. He had a dream. But my Daddy fought for the dream. And it was his right to fight for the dream. You have a Constitutional right, and that's what Daddy said, 'I have a right to bear arms. And if I need to protect my family,' especially when the police did not protect us, then he had a right to do that. The Deacons had a right to carry the guns."

> *"Even protesters who otherwise enjoy high levels of public support ... can lose support from the general public if they use violence."*

Violent Protests Don't Help the Cause

Melissa De Witte

Despite the best intentions of organizers, protests sometimes turn violent. In the following viewpoint, Melissa De Witte argues that can be bad not only for the individuals involved in the violence, but for the cause itself. The author reports on research by a sociologist at Stanford University showing that violent protests can cause the public to feel more supportive of those being protested against than of the protestors. Melissa De Witte is a public information officer at Stanford.

As you read, consider the following questions:

1. What inspired the researchers to do this study at this time?
2. How did the researchers set up the study?
3. What do the researchers describe as the limitations of their work?

"Violence by Protesters Can Lead the Public to Support Them Less, Stanford Sociologist Says," by Melissa De Witte, Stanford University, October 12, 2018. Reprinted by permission.

P rotesters are not helping their cause when they turn violent toward their opposition. In fact, their aggressions could increase support for the very people they're protesting against, according to new research by Stanford sociologist Robb Willer.

The research—inspired by recent confrontations between white nationalist protesters and anti-racist counter-protesters in Charlottesville, Virginia, and Berkeley, California—found that violence by anti-racist protesters can lead people to view them as unreasonable, a perception that may lead to people identifying less with the group. However, violence by white supremacists didn't change people's opinion because they already saw the white supremacists as extremely unreasonable, said Robb Willer in a paper published Oct. 11 in *Socius: Sociological Research for a Dynamic World*.

Brent Simpson of the University of South Carolina and Matthew Feinberg of the University of Toronto are co-authors on the paper.

When anti-racists turn their protest into violence it can backfire even further: In some cases, it can influence support for the other side, said Willer.

"Our central finding is that even protesters who otherwise enjoy high levels of public support—anti-racist activists counter-protesting a gathering of white nationalists—can lose support from the general public if they use violence," said Willer. "In fact, we found that support for white nationalists was heightened among those who read that anti-racist counter-protesters had attacked them."

The Rise of Violent Protest

Violent protests have become more common in the U.S. since the 2016 election, noted Willer and his co-authors.

"There's been rising diversity of protest tactics, including the use of violence," said Willer. "Given that people typically react very negatively to violence, my co-authors and I were curious about public reactions to violent protest. Are protesters who use

AGENT PROVOCATEUR

As a young activist, I was eager to learn the lessons available from previous movement experience as quickly as possible—I didn't want to learn the hard way by making all the mistakes myself. Whenever Martin Luther King Jr.'s senior advisor Bayard Rustin came to town, I could be found sitting at his feet. That went for Bayard's own mentor A.J. Muste, too—and one of Muste's stories seems particularly relevant in this moment.

At one point Muste found himself chairing the strike committee for a militant trade union, and he became curious about a member of the committee who persistently argued for violent tactics to defend against the violence that was escalating against the workers. Muste did some sleuthing, and discovered that the man was being paid to incite the workers to turn to violent tactics. So he "outed" the man, and the union remained nonviolent in response to the violence against them—which ultimately led their strike to victory.

That story was eye-opening: those who want our struggles to fail may want us to turn to violence, figuring then we're more likely to lose. It's useful for them to persuade or hire an "agent provocateur" (a French phrase because this is an international phenomenon) to turn a just movement to violence.

At this moment in U.S. history there's a rapid growth of social movements clamoring for change. The guardians of the status quo are bound to feel threatened, and as they lose ground they're likely to be tempted to use agent provocateurs to turn us violent. Just in time, nonviolent researcher Steve Chase has produced a short handbook for us that responds to this problem: *How Agent Provocateurs Harm Our Movements: Some Historical Examples and a Few Ideas on Reducing the Risk*. Steve tells stories from the United States, Central America, Thailand, Syria, Sudan, Poland, China, the United Kingdom and Canada—all countries where agent provocateurs have tried (sometimes successfully) to turn nonviolent movements violent.

violence turning off the general public, inadvertently making their opponents more credible?"

To study how people perceive violence in public protest and civil resistance, Willer surveyed 800 people recruited online.

The survey was split into four conditions: Depending on the experiment, participants read one of four newspaper articles. While based on protests that took place in Charlottesville and Berkeley in August 2017, elements of the stories were fabricated for experimental control.

In one scenario, participants read a news story about white nationalists who staged a protest of the removal of Confederate monuments. In the report, a group of anti-racists showed up to stage a counter-demonstration. It was made clear that neither group was violent. In the other three conditions, the article portrayed violence by one group or the other or both.

For example, in the news report in which anti-racist counter-protesters were violent, it read: "One white nationalist was knocked to the ground by counter-protesters carrying homemade shields," that "a counter-protester was seen punching and kicking a white nationalist who lay on the ground shielding his face from the blows," and that "the anti-racism counter-protesters [...] pepper-sprayed white nationalists."

Participants were then asked how they perceived the violence that occurred, as well as questions about their attitudes toward and support for the two groups.

Willer found that when the anti-racist group alone was violent, participants perceived them as less reasonable and identified with them less. Participants also showed less support for the anti-racist group and increased support for the people they were violent against: the white nationalists.

However, when white nationalists were violent, it did not lead to increased support for anti-racist movements overall.

"We found that white nationalist protesters who used violence were not perceived as less reasonable and did not lose support, because they were already seen as extremely unreasonable and were strongly opposed," said Willer. "When compared to their anti-racist opponents who could lose support if they used violence, this highlights an interesting asymmetry in the likely consequences of violent protest."

The Risks of Violent Protest

Because white nationalists are a widely despised group known for violence, they have little to lose if they can draw out violence from anti-racists.

"Violence did little, if any, damage to their reputations," said the researchers in the paper. "Conversely, violence by anti-racists can not only damage public support for anti-racists; as our results show, it can also increase support for the white nationalist protesters themselves."

Willer hopes that for activists concerned with popular support for their movement, these findings can help them understand the value of ensuring protests remain peaceful.

"It is important to acknowledge limitations of our work," said Willer. "Violence cannot always be avoided, such as when it is used in self-defense. But our results do fit well with other work suggesting that violent activism typically turns people off, including potential supporters, and that it builds opposition to those who use it. If people understood clearly the effects of violent protest on public opinion, they might try harder to convince other activists on their side not to use these tactics."

> *"Darkness cannot drive out darkness: only light can do that. Hate cannot drive out hate: only love can do that."*

The Leader of One of the Most Successful Protest Movements of Our Time Was Committed to Nonviolence

Stanford University

This viewpoint from the Martin Luther King, Jr. Research and Education Institute at Stanford University outlines how King came to his views about nonviolence and how he applied his commitment to nonviolence to the civil rights movement as well as to other issues the world confronted. The Martin Luther King, Jr. Research and Education Institute supports a broad range of educational activities illuminating Dr. King's life and the movements he inspired.

As you read, consider the following questions:

1. What, according to the viewpoint, were the primary influences on Dr. King's philosophy of nonviolence?
2. Why did some civil rights leaders, such as Stokely Carmichael, begin to reject nonviolence?
3. Why did King believe that refusing to hate the opponent was as important as refusing to shoot them?

As a theologian, Martin Luther King reflected often on his understanding of nonviolence. He described his own "pilgrimage to nonviolence" in his first book, *Stride Toward Freedom*, and in subsequent books and articles. "True pacifism," or "nonviolent resistance," King wrote, is "a courageous confrontation of evil by the power of love" (King, *Stride*, 80). Both "morally and practically" committed to nonviolence, King believed that "the Christian doctrine of love operating through the Gandhian method of nonviolence was one of the most potent weapons available to oppressed people in their struggle for freedom" (King, *Stride*, 79; *Papers* 5:422).

King was first introduced to the concept of nonviolence when he read Henry David Thoreau's *Essay on Civil Disobedience* as a freshman at Morehouse College. Having grown up in Atlanta and witnessed segregation and racism every day, King was "fascinated by the idea of refusing to cooperate with an evil system" (King, *Stride*, 73).

In 1950, as a student at Crozer Theological Seminary, King heard a talk by Dr. Mordecai Johnson, president of Howard University. Dr. Johnson, who had recently traveled to India, spoke about the life and teachings of Mohandas K. Gandhi. Gandhi, King later wrote, was the first person to transform Christian love into a powerful force for social change. Gandhi's stress on love and nonviolence gave King "the method for social reform that I had been seeking" (King, *Stride*, 79).

While intellectually committed to nonviolence, King did not experience the power of nonviolent direct action first-hand until the start of the Montgomery bus boycott in 1955. During the boycott, King personally enacted Gandhian principles. With guidance from black pacifist Bayard Rustin and Glenn Smiley of the Fellowship of Reconciliation, King eventually decided not to use armed bodyguards despite threats on his life, and reacted to violent experiences, such as the bombing of his home, with compassion. Through the practical experience of leading nonviolent protest, King came to understand how nonviolence could become a way of life, applicable to all situations. King called the principle of nonviolent resistance the "guiding light of our movement. Christ furnished the spirit and motivation while Gandhi furnished the method" (*Papers* 5:423).

King's notion of nonviolence had six key principles. First, one can resist evil without resorting to violence. Second, nonviolence seeks to win the "friendship and understanding" of the opponent, not to humiliate him (King, *Stride*, 84). Third, evil itself, not the people committing evil acts, should be opposed. Fourth, those committed to nonviolence must be willing to suffer without retaliation as suffering itself can be redemptive. Fifth, nonviolent resistance avoids "external physical violence" and "internal violence of spirit" as well: "The nonviolent resister not only refuses to shoot his opponent but he also refuses to hate him" (King, *Stride*, 85). The resister should be motivated by love in the sense of the Greek word *agape*, which means "understanding," or "redeeming good will for all men" (King, *Stride*, 86). The sixth principle is that the nonviolent resister must have a "deep faith in the future," stemming from the conviction that "the universe is on the side of justice" (King, *Stride*, 88).

During the years after the bus boycott, King grew increasingly committed to nonviolence. An India trip in 1959 helped him connect more intimately with Gandhi's legacy. King began to advocate nonviolence not just in a national sphere, but internationally as well: "the potential destructiveness of modern weapons" convinced King that "the choice today is no longer between violence and nonviolence. It is either nonviolence or nonexistence" (*Papers* 5:424).

After Black Power advocates such as Stokely Carmichael began to reject nonviolence, King lamented that some African Americans had lost hope, and reaffirmed his own commitment to nonviolence: "Occasionally in life one develops a conviction so precious and meaningful that he will stand on it till the end. This is what I have found in nonviolence" (King, *Where*, 63–64). He wrote in his 1967 book, *Where Do We Go from Here: Chaos or Community?*: "We maintained the hope while transforming the hate of traditional revolutions into positive nonviolent power. As long as the hope was fulfilled there was little questioning of nonviolence. But when the hopes were blasted, when people came to see that in spite of progress their conditions were still insufferable … despair began to set in" (King, *Where*, 45). Arguing that violent revolution was impractical in the context of a multiracial society, he concluded: "Darkness cannot drive out darkness: only light can do that. Hate cannot drive out hate: only love can do that. The beauty of nonviolence is that in its own way and in its own time it seeks to break the chain reaction of evil" (King, *Where*, 62–63).

Footnotes

King, "Pilgrimage to Nonviolence," 13 April 1960, in *Papers* 5:419–425.
King, *Stride Toward Freedom*, 1958.
King, *Where Do We Go from Here*, 1967.

> *"Where people don't believe their appeals to authorities will be heard, protesters may be more likely to adopt violent methods of protest. Under these circumstances, people think they have 'nothing to lose.'"*

Heavy-Handed Policing Can Cause Peaceful Protests to Turn Violent

Emma Thomas

As we've already seen in this chapter, there is evidence that violent protests are not effective. Yet still, protests often do turn violent. In the following viewpoint, Emma Thomas looks at why this happens. She finds that people who are likely to resort to violence are psychologically different from those who aren't, as well as being involved in the cause for different reasons. But ultimately, the response from authorities might be what makes the difference between a protest remaining peaceful or not. Emma Thomas is associate professor in the School of Psychology at Flinders University in Australia.

As you read, consider the following questions:

1. According to this viewpoint, how does aggressive police response aid in turning protests violent?
2. How do online interactions contribute to feelings of anger that lead to protests?
3. How did the killing of George Floyd affect people in other countries?

We have seen ten days of protests in the United States over the death of George Floyd.

While thousands of people have gathered to express their outrage peacefully, some demonstrations have been marred by vandalism and violent clashes with police.

Research has shown that people generally see confrontational protests as unwarranted and ineffectual.

So why do some protests turn violent? And as we watch this mass movement gather pace around the world, what makes people come out into the streets in the first place?

Why Do Some Protests Turn Violent?

Research suggests people who are prepared to use violent confrontation can be psychologically different from those who are not. People who are prepared to adopt violence are more likely to report feelings of contempt for political adversaries whom they hold responsible for wrongdoing.

In the US, some commentators have suggested the violence on their streets stems from a deep sense of despair and helplessness that things never change.

Psychological research offers some support for this analysis. Where people don't believe their appeals to authorities will be heard, protesters may be more likely to adopt violent methods of protest.

Under these circumstances, people think they have "nothing to lose."

Heavy-Handed Policing Can Lead to Violence

However, there is another key element here. Feelings of contempt and helplessness do not arise in a vacuum—they stem from real-world interactions between people and groups.

We know from decades of research into policing and crowds that violent, heavy-handed treatment from the police is a major catalyst of protest violence. Such experiences lead people to redefine their understanding of the demonstrating group's purpose.

Over the past week, people who initially turned out to express their constitutional right to protest peacefully have found they are now enemies of the state—dissidents in their own country. Under these circumstances, the purpose of the protest suddenly adopts a much broader meaning.

Protesters Can Change Their Tactics

A good way to make people feel contempt is to disregard their safety and purpose.

So, even though people tend to think confrontational protests do not work, our research shows that their assessment changes when an authority is seen to be corrupt and immoral.

Put differently, even the average punter may come to see violence as more acceptable if the state responds in a way that seems unjustified and disproportionate.

Why Do People Protest in the First Place?

Given the recent restrictions on public gatherings, who could have imagined that we would be witnessing a global solidarity movement of this scale in the middle of a deadly pandemic?

It has long been observed that specific events can serve as tipping points that catalyse social movements. Consider the actions of US activist Rosa Parks, who famously refused to give up her seat to a white man on an Alabama bus in 1955, inspiring mass resistance to the racial segregation policies of the time.

When Tunisian fruit seller Mohamed Bouazizi set himself on fire in response to police corruption and harassment in December

2010, his actions were broadcast all over the world, laying the foundation of the mass protests that would become the Arab Spring.

Research shows people who engage in protest do so because they feel angry about injustices perpetrated against groups they are committed to and believe they can make a difference by acting collectively.

Critically, in the 21st century, specific events—and our reactions to them—can now be broadcast online and shared with millions of people, across the world, within a matter of hours.

Online Interactions Generate Outrage and Common Purpose

These online interactions are more than just chatter. Research shows online interactions about injustice can be the very means through which people's protest commitments are formed and maintained.

As people interact online, it generates a sense of shared outrage, as well as a belief that if "we" act together, things could be different.

Research has specifically shown that people who interact online about the police killings of Black people are more likely to attend protests, especially if they live in an area with historically high rates of police killings of Black people.

What Does This Mean for Australia?

The George Floyd protest movement has also reached Australia.

There have already been a number of peaceful demonstrations around Australia to protest Indigenous deaths in custody and support Black Lives Matter. More are planned for the weekend.

How Australians respond to racism in our own country is a matter for Australians in our own individual and collective ways.

But authorities should take note: heavy-handed responses from police can provoke more violent responses from otherwise peaceful protesters.

Periodical and Internet Sources Bibliography

The following articles have been selected to supplement the diverse views presented in this chapter.

Laura Bassett, "Why Violent Protests Work," *GQ*, June 2, 2020. https://www.gq.com/story/why-violent-protests-work.

Erica Chenoweth and Maria J. Stephan, "Violence Is a Dangerous Route for Protestors," *Foreign Policy*, December 18, 2019. https://foreignpolicy.com/2019/12/18/violent-resistance-protests-nonviolence/.

Isaac Chotiner, "How Violent Protests Change Politics," *New Yorker*, May 29, 2020. https://www.newyorker.com/news/q-and-a/how-violent-protests-change-politics.

John Horgan, "The Problem with Protesting Violence with Violence," *Scientific American*, June 2, 2020. https://blogs.scientificamerican.com/cross-check/the-problem-with-protesting-violence-with-violence/.

César Jiménez-Martínez, "Media, Protest, and the Simplification of Violence," Media@LSE (London School of Economics), July 13, 2020. https://blogs.lse.ac.uk/medialse/2020/07/13/media-protest-and-the-simplification-of-violence/.

Francine Mends, MD, "Why Polite, Peaceful Protest Doesn't Work," Medium, June 10, 2020. https://medium.com/fearless-she-wrote/why-polite-peaceful-protest-doesnt-work-2936f299eb12.

Tonya Mosley and Allison Hagan, "Violence as a Form of Protest," WBUR, June 11, 2020. https://www.wbur.org/hereandnow/2020/06/11/voilence-protests-racial-justice.

Michelle Nicholasen, "Nonviolent Resistance Proves Potent Weapon," *Harvard Gazette*, February 4, 2019. https://news.harvard.edu/gazette/story/2019/02/why-nonviolent-resistance-beats-violent-force-in-effecting-social-political-change/.

Tina Rosenberg, "A Dissenter's Legacy: How to Win Without Violence," *New York Times*, February 6, 2018. https://www.nytimes.com/2018/02/06/opinion/a-dissenters-legacy-how-to-win-without-violence.html.

Thomas J. Sugrue, "2020 Is Not 1968: To Understand Today's Protests, You Must Look Further Back," *National Geographic*, June 11, 2020. https://www.nationalgeographic.com/history/article/2020 -not-1968.

Brenda Valdivia and Michael Hagerty, "In Moments of Great Social Change, America Has a History of Violence," Houston Public Media, June 10, 2020. https://www.houstonpublicmedia.org /articles/shows/houston-matters/2020/06/10/375391/in -moments-of-great-social-change-america-has-a-history-of -violence/.

James Melvin Washington, ed. "Nonviolence: The Only Road to Freedom," in *A Testament of Hope: The Essential Writings and Speeches of Martin Luther King, Jr.* San Francisco, CA: Harper San Francisco, 1986.

CHAPTER 3

Do Protest Movements Require Charismatic Leaders?

Chapter Preface

T he twenty-first century has been a century of protests, many if not most of them worldwide. Some made international headlines; others were less well-known outside of their communities. But one thing that is interesting is how no single leader of the magnitude of Martin Luther King Jr. or Mahatma Gandhi has emerged. This has not been an accident, and it's possibly not a defect.

Though it was probably not the first de-centralized social movement, Occupy Wall Street was likely the first to actively intend and embrace that strategy. Other movements, such as the Black Lives Matter movement, have largely followed that game plan. It might be the case that in today's easily connected world, where a movement can start in one city and quickly engulf a region or the world, and where individual members of a movement can easily communicate with each other and the press, strong central leadership is doomed. But is this a failure or an advantage? That is what the viewpoint authors in this chapter discuss.

Here you will find reporting on research into the leadership styles of social movements and what effects those movements have had. You will hear opinions about what motivates protesters to pour into the streets to risk their freedom and sometimes their lives, and opinions about what can sap that motivation when there is insufficient management at the higher levels of the movement. And you will read how good leadership might be crucial for keeping peaceful protests from turning violent. You will learn the importance of defined goals and a cohesive strategy in creating an effective social movement. The closing viewpoint looks not at a leader, but at another motivating factor: a powerful image.

> *"On April 12, Kataguiri's Free Brazil Movement and associated groups fielded protests in 200 cities across Brazil, the largest country in Latin America and the fifth biggest in the world."*

Good Protest Leaders Must Be Willing to Employ Modern Tactics

Lawrence W. Reed

In the following viewpoint, Lawrence W. Reed spotlights Kim Kataguiri, a teen activist from Brazil who led the Free Brazil Movement in that country. Reed argues that young Kataguiri, who is now a member of Brazil's Congress, was exactly the kind of leader needed to effect change. Lawrence W. Reed is the Foundation for Economic Education's President Emeritus, Humphreys Family Senior Fellow, and Ron Manners Global Ambassador for Liberty, having served for nearly 11 years as FEE's president.

As you read, consider the following questions:

1. Why did Thomas Jefferson like rebellion?
2. What was Kataguiri's group protesting in Brazil?
3. What political philosophy do Kataguiri and the author endorse?

"Millions in Brazil Follow a Teen Leader to Freedom," by Lawrence W. Reed, Foundation for Economic Education, June 4, 2015. https://fee.org/articles/millions-in-brazil-follow-a -teen-leader-to-freedom. Licensed under a CC BY-4.0 International.

I like a little rebellion now and then," Thomas Jefferson famously wrote. The primary author of the Declaration of Independence and America's third president regarded rebellion as "like a storm in the atmosphere." It clears the air and settles matters.

A storm is brewing in the Brazilian political atmosphere at this very moment. Amazingly, the hero at the center of it is not a seasoned veteran of government, media, business, or labor. He is not a Marxist, a class warfare demagogue, or a bomb-thrower. He'd sooner spit on a Che Guevara T-shirt than wear one. He's a 19-year-old college dropout with a very un-Brazilian last name, and he's a libertarian—one that Jefferson himself likely would embrace with enthusiasm. Meet Kim Kataguiri, the cofounder and public face of the Free Brazil Movement.

Just two years ago, this grandson of Japanese immigrants was a high school student with no political profile, public or private. His story is a perfect example of something we at the Foundation for Economic Education (FEE) frequently identify as essential to the future of liberty: packaging our ideas in ways young people find both accessible and exciting, and then putting them out there in venues that young people use.

When attractive ideas converge with catalyzing events and strong personalities, big and unpredictable things happen. In hindsight, we see clearly that the demise of communism in one country after another in 1989 resulted from such a perfect alignment. In Brazil, the rise of libertarian ideas is so palpable that the statist left is having fits trying to finger some evil puppet master behind it all. As in the United States, the statists can't conceive of a decentralized, ideas-based, grassroots movement of people who actually believe passionately in freedom and free markets; to them, the opposition is always a nefarious conspiracy of a few. The catalyzing events behind Brazil's freedom movement are high taxes, massive corruption and cronyism, rising price inflation amid a sluggish economy, and the widely perceived incompetence of President Dilma Rousseff and her socialist-leaning Workers' Party.

"I learned about Milton Friedman and Ludwig von Mises through the Internet," Kataguiri told me in a June 2 interview. He cited a think tank headquartered in Sao Paulo, Mises Institute-Brazil, as one source of those ideas. Another was Portal Libertarianismo. I take special pride in this revelation from him: "A lot of articles from the FEE website were translated by these Brazilian libertarians and have helped tens of thousands of people to know the ideas of liberty."

In neighboring Argentina, people take to the streets for almost any cause. Brazilians are more laid back. So on March 15, 2015, when Kataguiri and his young associates turned out nearly two million Brazilians in 25 cities to protest corruption and socialism, a sensation was born. Helio Beltrao, founder and president of Mises Institute-Brazil, sees Kataguiri as "a natural, dynamic leader." On April 12, Kataguiri's Free Brazil Movement and associated groups fielded protests in 200 cities across Brazil, the largest country in Latin America and the fifth biggest in the world. Beltrao says, "The left is completely in awe over this. These were the largest demonstrations of any kind, for any reason, since at least 1992 in our country."

A key ingredient in Kataguiri's success so far is his mastery of video and social media. He's prolific, eloquent—and some say delightfully "quirky"—on Facebook, Twitter, and YouTube. Reportedly, Rousseff and her minions are outraged and embarrassed at the effectiveness of his incisive barbs. He and his Free Brazil Movement have even engineered classes and rock concerts with free-market themes. Drawing comparisons to the early days of the Arab Spring, the left-leaning Brazilian press has found these ingenious efforts impossible to ignore.

What caused this teenager to morph so quickly from a studious high schooler to a nationally admired activist whose name is now known by a large portion of Brazil's 200 million people?

"First of all," Kataguiri told me, "Rousseff's government increased the size of the state more than any other. The inflation and unemployment rates have reached historic levels. Her government is up to its neck in corruption scandals that not only steal the population's money but use it to buy the Congress. Today, only 7 percent of the Brazilian people approve of the government. It's very clear that the statist model of the Workers' Party has failed the country. Every political party in Brazil steals our money, but only the Workers' Party uses our money to steal our freedom."

The precipitous decline in Rousseff's popularity is especially remarkable given that she won reelection (though narrowly) just eight months ago. The burst of libertarian pressure may be partly responsible for her recent attempts to reverse course. In small ways, her administration has begun to cut government spending and call for reining in out-of-control entitlement programs. She vociferously denies any personal involvement in the burgeoning corruption at the state-owned oil company, Petrobras. But those efforts so far have earned mostly disdain from her base and cries of "too little, too late" from others, including Kataguiri. The air is thick with calls for her impeachment even though Brazilian law makes that prospect extremely problematic.

I asked Kataguiri if his notoriety has caused him any personal troubles. "I've been threatened several times by people and organizations paid by the government, but I'm not afraid," he said. "I knew from the very beginning of our Free Brazil Movement that we would be fighting against criminals. Someone had to do that, and now that millions of people are putting their hopes on me, I can't give up. What the people want now is less government and more money in their own pockets where it belongs."

No matter where the impeachment effort may go, this new libertarianism in Brazil seems solidly ensconced and poised for growth. "I expect that in the next decade or two, most of our society will not only understand classical liberalism, but defend it too."

Beltrao agrees. In only the last month, his organization has spearheaded the creation of the Liberty Network (Rede Liberdade), bringing together many liberty-leaning think tanks and organizations in Brazil to share ideas and strategies and to collaborate on public activities. It gained significant attention on

June 1 when it organized a campaign against taxes that make up 60 percent of the price of beer. And though no political party in Brazil has been committed to liberty since the 19th century, one is now in the making. The Novo ("New") Party has gathered the signatures necessary for the next step: certification by the government so it can field candidates in elections.

Kataguiri and his comrades are refreshingly principled. When they speak of free enterprise, they don't mean crony capitalism. When they call for reductions in spending, they include social programs. They realize that social programs are little more than attempts by corrupt politicians to buy votes with the voters' own money. They quote Bastiat, Mises, Friedman, and Hayek.

When you're already a hero at 19, just imagine where you might be when you're 30! William Pitt was prime minister of Great Britain at age 24. I predict that we will hear the name of Kim Kataguiri for a long time to come.

> "*Many protests that have shaken the world in recent years ... have not pursued their aims in terms of rights, but instead in terms of economic justice and the need for real democracy.*"

A Desire for Democracy and Economic Justice Motivates Modern Protests

Sara Burke

In the following viewpoint, Sara Burke analyzes research that seeks to characterize protests that emerged from 2006 to 2013 in many different parts of the world. The protests were largely bottom-up responses driven not by charismatic leadership but by populations who felt their voices were not being heard by those in power, whether those were despots or democratically elected leaders. Sara Burke is senior policy analyst at the Friedrich Ebert Foundation, a foundation associated with the Social Democratic Party of Germany.

"What an Era of Global Protests Says About the Effectiveness of Human Rights as a Language to Achieve Social Change," by Sara Burke, *International Journal on Human Rights*, December 2014. Reprinted by permission.

As you read, consider the following questions:

1. What was the main thrust of the grievances that sparked the protests analyzed by the report discussed in the viewpoint?
2. According to the author, what problem does the human rights field have when it comes to articulating their demands?
3. What is at the root of protesters' demands?

In recent years, the world has been shaken by protests, peaceful and otherwise. The Arab Spring, the anti-austerity protests throughout Europe, Occupy and the movement of the Squares around the world are well known to us because of the extensive international media coverage they have received. These protests were largely non-violent, but recent years have seen violent protests as well, with a particular spike in 2007–08 due to riots over food prices; these protests are less well covered in international news. Compounding recent years of unrest, in which hot spots of civil war and armed conflict have also continued, there has been an increasing failure of existing political arrangements at the local, national and global levels to address grievances raised by protesters in a peaceful, just and orderly way. It is therefore of the utmost importance to understand what is driving recent protests, and in particular to do so on a global level.

This was the contention behind research contributing to "World Protests 2006–2013",[1] which queried over 500 local and international news sources available on the Internet to analyse 843 protest events (both non-violent and violent, organized and spontaneous), occurring between January 2006 and July 2013 in 84 countries covering over 90% of the world population. Researchers looked for evidence of main grievances and demands, who is protesting, what methods they use, who their opponents or targets are and what results from protests, including achievements and repression. The objective of the study was to document and characterize manifestations of protest from just before the onset of the recent world economic crisis to the present, to examine protest trends globally, regionally and according to country income levels, and to present the main grievances and demands of protesters in order to better understand the drivers of social unrest. The objective of the present article is to ask what light the findings of this study may shed upon one of the existential questions for human rights as posed by the editors of this 10th Anniversary issue of *SUR*: Is human rights (still) an effective language for producing social change?

"World Protests 2006–2013" finds that the trend of outrage and discontent expressed in protests may be increasing worldwide. The leading cause of all protests is a cluster of grievances related to economic justice and against austerity policies that includes demands to reform public services and pensions; to create good jobs and better labour conditions; make tax collection and fiscal spending progressive; reduce or eliminate inequality; alleviate low-living standards; enact land reform; and ensure affordable food, energy and housing. Although broad demands for economic justice are numerous and widespread, the single demand that exceeds all others is found in a cluster of grievances pointing to a failure of political representation. It points to the very issue that prevents progress toward economic justice: a lack of real democracy

As the key grievance in a widespread crisis of political systems, the demand for real democracy is counter-posed by many protesters to formal, representative democracy, which is increasingly faulted around the world for serving elites and private interests. The study found demands not just for better governance and wider representation, but also for universal direct participation and a society in which democratic principles—liberty, equality, justice and solidarity—are found not only in the laws and institutions but in everyday life (ERREJÓN, 2013; HARDT; NEGRI, 2004; RANCIÈRE, 2006). This demand comes from protesters in a variety of political systems, and protest patterns indicate that not only authoritarian governments, but also representative democracies, both old and new, are failing to hear and respond to the needs of a majority of citizens.

Grievances expressed as rights-based by protesters are one of the main groups identified in the study, but they are significantly fewer in number than those related to economic justice. Rights-based grievances and demands are also behind fewer protests than grievances related to failure of political representation or global justice. In the study, rights-based grievances are identified for human rights, civil and political rights such as freedom of assembly, speech and the press, and also for the social and cultural rights of ethnic groups, immigrant groups, indigenous, LGBT, prisoners, racial, religious and women's groups (including protests for the revocation of existing rights). The study also notes some protests for rights that are both economic and civil/political, namely labour rights and the right to the Commons (digital, land, cultural, atmospheric). However, the economic justice demands that have dominated world protests since 2006 have not formulated themselves primarily in the language of rights or sought their realization primarily through national legislation of international norms, according to the findings of the study. Why might this be? Both a realpolitik examination of the powers and interests on both sides and a critical examination of the framing of economic rights, as compared to civil and political rights, offer some insight.

With regard to the realpolitik issue of power dynamics, the study finds that middle-class protesters of all ages, from students to retired pensioners, are increasingly joining activists from various movements. Not only in sanctioned marches and rallies, but in a new framework of protest that includes acts with greater potential consequences, including civil disobedience and direct actions such as road blockages, occupations of city streets and squares, and mass educational events and "happenings" to raise awareness about issues like debt, fair taxation for public services and inequality. The impact of people's feeling about inequalities should not be underestimated in understanding what has driven many protests, particularly of the middle classes, in recent years.

Even in a country that has seen policy-driven success in combating high inequality, such as Brazil, it has not proven enough to satisfy people's demands, as seen during the summer of 2013 with the evolution of protests from localized demands for affordable public transportation to national demands for sweeping changes in social protection, distribution of wealth and government corruption.

The other side of the power dynamic concerns the opponents of these protesters. The study finds, not surprisingly, that the target of most protests is the national government in the country where the protest occurs.[2] Many protests also explicitly denounce the international political and economic system, the influence of corporations and the privilege of elites, including the financial sector. A large number of protests against austerity implicate the International Monetary Fund and European Central Bank, which are widely perceived as the chief architects and advocates of austerity. The challenge faced by protesters is achieving not just social change, but social *justice*. And doing it against the interests of a powerful nexus of poorly-representative governments and captured international financial institutions dominated by private corporate and financial elites, all of which are complicit in upholding an economic system that produces and reproduces inequality (of great concern to the middle classes) and privation (of ongoing concern to the world's poorest). The repression experienced by protesters seeking economic justice offers further insight into the challenges they face and therefore the modes and methods of protest they have adopted. Not only riots, but more than half of all protests, experience some sort of repression in terms of arrests, injuries or deaths at the hands of authorities, or subsequent surveillance of suspected protesters and groups—surveillance that is carried out by both governments and private corporations.

This state of affairs has been long in the making. Falling wages and shrinking pensions led to decades of rising inequalities and decreasing opportunities for decent work and full engagement in society, especially for youth, which has paved the way for the joining of middle class protesters with unemployed and precarious workers over this period. Of the protests linked to economic policy—either arising in response to a policy implementation or law or demanding policy changes—the greatest number are in relation to subsidies, typically a threat to remove a subsidy for fuel or food. A great number also relate to labor compensation and regulation of safety in the workplace, taxes and financial regulation, and fiscal and social security policies. A smaller number pertain to attempts at non-financial regulation and international tax cooperation. These protests are largely a response to the unravelling of the social contract that formerly bound the world's middle classes more tightly to the policies of elites, including remnants of the welfare state. This unravelling contributes to a mounting failure of existing political arrangements at the local, national and global levels to deal with problems and protests peacefully and justly. The world's people are roiled by economic needs that go unaddressed because they are, in ever greater numbers, shut out of the political processes in which decisions about the economy are made. Furthermore, they are shut out by the very elites who benefit directly from those decisions.

Can human rights norms and agreements be an effective weapon against such an adversary when its economic interests are at stake? Inequality, to a degree world protests indicate is unacceptable, is this adversary's stated intention. This adversary counters all objections with imperatives: to prioritize growth and deregulation, low debt-to-GDP ratios, the rights of creditors and the privileged role owed to private interests in the economy and government. Could it be that the success of the Occupy and *Indignants* movements in changing the discourse around inequality lies in their resistance to formulating demands as a list of policies to be put to such authorities?

This was philosopher Judith Butler's contention in a 2012 essay entitled "So What Are the Demands?", referring to the question repeatedly directed to the Occupy movement, which resisted giving a straight answer. Butler points out that even the most comprehensive list of demands—including for example, jobs for

The World Needs Leaders

It is very useful for a movement or a country to have charismatic leaders. There are many historic examples, just to name Mohandas Gandhi or Martin Luther King, where you had the leaders running the movements, being an inspiration, being a strategist, being a philosopher, being public figures, being CEOs of these movements.

Then you have another set of movements where you have a more symbolic role of leadership. You want to name Nelson Mandela, who was sitting in jail for so long; Aung San Suu Kyi obviously spending years under house arrest in Burma; but they were an inspiration to their people.

Now you are witnessing the completely new breed of movements, even called leaderless movements. So you have this kind of hidden leadership that operates the movement, and people don't want to be seen, whether because the people lost faith in traditional leadership in the society or they are just afraid that the government will come and kill them all. But in any case, you really don't see the charismatic leaders.

But leadership is needed. Leadership is needed in nonviolent movements, leadership is needed in successful countries. There are so many roles of leadership. Whether we are talking about individual leaders or group leadership, there must be somebody to lead these movements, there must be somebody to formulate the vision, there must be somebody to achieve the unity, there must be somebody taking credit or giving other credit for success, there must be somebody taking the responsibility for mistakes. That's the basic role of leadership. So the world needs a lot of leadership.

The good news is that you need a little bit of talent to be a leader, but, like in music, like when you are playing a violin, the talent is only part of the deal. You can train people in leadership skills, and leadership skills are transferable. There must be an effort to make those leadership skills more available to the people.

I have met so many different groups. We work with groups from 46 different countries. You can't imagine the kind of talented young people in their early 20s that I have met in the craziest countries of this world. They must be equipped with the toolbox to emerge as real leaders, because, believe me, the talent is there.

"Leadership and Nonviolent Movements," by Srdja Popovic, Carnegie Council.

all, an end to foreclosures and forgiveness of student debt and so on—cannot but fail to express the movement's ultimate ambition to resist inequality. This is so, she argues, because such a list can never communicate how those demands are related, and an end to inequality cannot be seen as simply one demand among many, but as the overarching frame. The problem requires instead a unifying and systemic approach (BUTLER, 2012).

Ironically, in spite of the principle that all human rights are indivisible and interdependent, the human rights field lacks a unified approach to economic, social and cultural rights, on the one hand, and civil and political rights, on the other. Progress in civil and political rights, the so-called "first-generation" human rights, such as the right to assembly, speech and religion, is largely based upon monitoring the relatively unambiguous presence or absence of negative outcomes (e.g. incidences of wrongful incarceration or censorship), whereas progress in economic, social and cultural rights, the "second-generation" of human rights, monitors their progressive realization over time (United Nations, 2012). In the case of economic rights, this is done via economic indicators that many protesters would find inaccessible because of their technical nature.

Excellent work has been done by a number of economists to rethink macroeconomics from a human rights perspective, including the model audits of US and Mexican economic policies conducted by Radhika Balakrishnan, Diane Elson and Raj Patel in 2009 for compliance with human rights obligations (BALAKRISHNAN; ELSON; PATEL, 2009), and the Outcomes, Policy Efforts and Resources to make an overall Assessment (OPERA) Framework developed in 2012 by the Center for Economic and Social Rights and their partners to create an overarching way for advocates and activists to build a well-evidenced argument about a state's level of compliance (CORKERY; WAY; WISNIEWSKI, 2012). Despite this work, doubts remain about the usefulness of using human rights to fight economic injustice precisely because these are legal and policy-based goals that require responsive democracies with meaningful citizen participation, which is the very problem blocking progress toward more equitable economic systems.

Perhaps this is why these path-breaking human rights economists are also modest in their goals, aiming less for radical change than to "move economic policy in a better direction by identifying which policies are at least likely to be inconsistent with human rights obligations" (BALAKRISHNAN; ELSON; PATEL, 2009). While their work remains an excellent guide for economic policy in real democracies, as a tool for the kind of system change that would actually fight further inequality, its value is sharply limited by political will.

The findings of the "World Protests 2006–2013" research and other efforts to map and understand the components of global protest—who is protesting and where, against which entities and with which methods, enduring what sort of repression and with what end results—should be of keen interest to those in the human rights field. They show that many protests that have shaken the world in recent years have framed their grievances as rights-based, but that the majority of protests, and those aiming specifically at changing the economic system—in particular its production and reproduction of inequality—have not pursued their aims in terms of rights, but instead in terms of economic justice and the need for real democracy. In conclusion, it is hoped that far-reaching and strategic thinkers within these protest movements, particularly those with the capacity to strategize on both a national and international level, will realize nonetheless that the advancement of human rights is necessary (if not sufficient) for the ultimate attainment of their goals.

Notes

1. September 2013 working paper by Isabel Ortiz, Director of Global Social Justice Program at Initiative for Policy Dialogue (IPD), Columbia University; Sara Burke, Senior Policy Analyst at Friedrich-Ebert-Stiftung New York (FES-NY); and research assistants Mohamed Berrada and Hernán Cortés, Ph.D. candidates in economics and international relations, respectively. Research was funded jointly by FES-NY and IPD. The paper can be downloaded at http://policydialogue.org/files/publications/World_Protests_2006-2013-Complete_and_Final_4282014.pdf. Last accessed on: 15 Aug. 2014.
2. Note: many protests have more than one target.

References

Balakrishnan, Radhika; Elson, Diane; Patel, Raj. 2009. Rethinking Macro Economic Strategies from a Human Rights Perspective. US Human Rights Network.

Butler, Judith. 2012. So, What Are the Demands? Title: Occupy Theory, Occupy Strategy. March. Available at: https://docs.google .com/file/d/0B8k8g5Bb3BxdbTNjZVJGa1NTXy1pTk4ycE1vTks wQQ/edit?pli=1. Last accessed on: 15 Aug. 2014.

Corkery, Allison; Way, Sally-Anne; Wisniewski, Victoria O. 2012. The Opera Framework: Assessing compliance with the obligation to fulfill economic, social and cultural rights. Center for Economic and Social Rights, Brooklyn, USA.

Errejón, Íñigo G. 2013. The People United Will Never Be Defeated: The M15 movement and the political crisis in Spain. In: Puschra, W.; Burke, S. (Orgs.). The Future We the People Need: Voices from New Social Movements in North Africa, Middle East, Europe & North America. New York: Friedrich-Ebert-Stiftung. Available at: http://library.fes.de/pdf-files/iez/global /09610-20130215.pdf. Last accessed on: 15 Aug. 2014.

Hardt, Michael; Negri, Antonio. 2004. Multitude: War and Democracy in the Age of Empire. New York: Penguin Books.

Ortiz, Isabel; Burke, Sara; Berrada, Mohamed; Cortés, Hernán. 2013. World Protest 2006-2013. IPD/FES Working Paper, New York. September. Available at: http://www.fes-globalization.org/new_ york/wp-content/uploads/2014/03/World-Protests-2006-2013 -Complete-and-Final.pdf. Last accessed on: Jul. 2014.

Rancière, Jacques. 2006. Hatred of Democracy. Translation: Corcoran, Steve. 2006. London: Verso.

United Nations. 2012. Office of the High Commissioner for Human Rights. Human Rights Indicators: Measurement and Implementation. UN Doc. HR/PUB/12/5/. Available at: http:// www.ohchr.org/Documents/Publications/Human_rights_ indicators_en.pdf. Last accessed on: 15 Aug. 2014.

> *"The very strength of the Black Lives Matter movement is that it is decentralized and a lot of the protest is more spontaneous. But that's also a weakness."*

Decentralization Is Both a Strength and a Weakness in Protest Movements

Melissa De Witte

In the following viewpoint, Melissa De Witte interviews Clayborne Carson, a historian of the civil rights movement and an expert on Dr. Martin Luther King Jr., about the role of leadership in protest movements and whether decentralized, leaderless movements can be effective. Dr. Carson points out the strengths and weaknesses of leaderless, decentralized protest movements. Melissa De Witte is a public information officer at Stanford University in Palo Alto, California.

As you read, consider the following questions:

1. How has the lack of centralized leadership been a weakness for the Black Lives Matter movement, according to Dr. Carson?
2. Why does Dr. Carson say that movements need leaders?
3. What role do leaders play in keeping protests peaceful, according to Dr. Carson's experience?

A s spontaneous and loosely organized demonstrations against the death of George Floyd continue to erupt across the world, Stanford historian and civil rights scholar Clayborne Carson has a message to activists: There needs to be some kind of leadership stating objectives of the current movement.

Unless goals are made clear by an articulate spokesperson, the movement may lose control of its messaging, Carson warns.

Here, Carson, a leading expert on the teachings of Dr. Martin Luther King Jr., reflects on what he has learned over a lifetime of protest and how today's demonstrations differ from the civil rights activism he participated in as a student at UCLA in 1965, including the infamous Watts Rebellion, a six-day riot in Los Angeles that resulted in 34 deaths, over 1,000 injuries, almost 4,000 arrests and $40 million in property damage.

Carson is the Martin Luther King, Jr., Centennial Professor of History in the School of Humanities and Sciences and the Ronnie Lott Founding Director of the Martin Luther King, Jr. Research and Education Institute. Carson's publications include *In Struggle: SNCC and the Black Awakening of the 1960s* (1981); *Malcolm X: The FBI File* (1991); *The Struggle for Freedom: A History of African Americans* (2005, 2010, co-author); and a memoir, *Martin's Dream: My Journey and the Legacy of Martin Luther King, Jr.* (2013).

What distinguishes these demonstrations from protests of the past?

Wherever there is a major stimulus for protest, something that outrages many people—for example, an unnecessary war (like all those during my adult life), or in this case, another video of a black man being killed by police—then there needs to be a way of expressing that outrage, either through nonviolent or violent methods. This happened after Rodney King's beating and Martin Luther King's assassination. It's probably the most positive way to spur those with authority to respond with a sense of urgency.

There has been a decade of protest about the issue of police brutality and the failure to punish police misbehavior. Established

BLACK LIVES MATTER: NO SINGLE LEADER, BUT HARDLY LEADERLESS

Instead of a pyramid of different departments topped by a leader, there is coordination and a set of shared values spread across a decentralized structure that prizes local connections and fast mobilization in response to police violence. Over the last eight years, the movement has steadily built a modern infrastructure on top of decades-old social justice institutions like the Highlander Center.

The distributed setup has at times contributed to tensions. National Black activists have feuded over which policy programs put forward by different organizations best represent the goals of the movement. Some admitted the decentralized system can confuse the public at times and leave the movement open to misconceptions in the press. But none of the 10 activists Politico spoke to from across the country said they wanted a hierarchical structure instead, as the movement seeks to turn its newfound momentum into policy changes at the local and national levels.

"In terms of strategy—and this is very real that we have to be honest about this—it makes it harder for those who are against us to do what they did in the '60s, which is to target one leader," said Cliff Albright, co-founder of Black Voters Matter Fund, a voter engagement nonprofit.

That doesn't make them leaderless, activists say. Instead, they call themselves "leaderful." Even at the beginning of the movement, the power structure was based in collaboration. The Black Lives Matter Global Network was co-founded in 2013 by three female organizers, and the Movement for Black Lives, formed one year later, has no governing board, though it coordinates with more than 150 organizations.

"Why the Black Lives Matter Movement Doesn't Want a Singular Leader," by Laura Barrón-López, Politico, July 22, 2020.

institutions, the police, the legal system as a whole, have failed. Sometimes justice delayed is justice denied, and that can fuel feelings of frustration.

For someone my age, who can remember a time when there were no cell phones, it was just me encountering a policeman who had the power to take my life. And whose word was going to be believed? In August 1965, I was in South Central Los Angeles during a rebellion that the press called the "Watts riot." Thirty-four people were killed as a result of "justifiable homicide." Compared to then, the police behaviors during these current protests have been relatively restrained. In that sense, there has been an obscenely modest bit of progress as rubber bullets have displaced lead bullets. But, if someone had told me in 1965 during Watts that my grandkids would still be subject to police executions, I would have thought I had failed in terms of trying to achieve change.

What makes a demonstration successful?

One thing that I think everyone would agree on is that the young people who are sparking these protests have no single charismatic, supremely articulate leader. One of the consequences is they don't control the messaging of it. I think that is one of the weaknesses of Black Lives Matter. There is no established leadership to articulate messages. What is the goal? Is it simply to express anger or is to achieve reform about police behavior? If it is to bring about reform, then what would that look like? It doesn't have to be one charismatic spokesperson. It could be many leaders, but there needs to be people saying, "This is what we want" and clearly articulating that. That's just not happening now with any consistency.

As a scholar of Dr. King, what do you think Dr. King would think about what is unfolding across the country? What advice do you think he would have?

I think he would be very pleased to see that the protests were not simply black people protesting. People who are not black are recognizing the urgency of the moment and the righteousness of the anger. I think he would also caution that some specific objectives should be clearly articulated. At some point, the anger and protest have to be linked to some concrete reforms, but I recognize that the protest organizers are reacting to recent events that could not be anticipated. The very strength of the Black Lives

Matter movement is that it is decentralized and a lot of the protest is more spontaneous. But that's also a weakness.

When you put this in the historical context of the demonstrations at the free speech movement and the civil rights demonstration of the mid-60s, the result in California was the election of Ronald Reagan as governor, which was certainly not the goal of the protest. But he presented himself as the law and order governor. It was similar with Richard Nixon. They come into office as the law and order presidents. Law and order is a potent political message, and I think protestors should notice that.

You said protests can be positive. What can be done to ensure they stay that way?

As a person who has probably been in hundreds of protests during my lifetime, I have watched demonstrations turn out badly and I have watched demonstrations turn out very peacefully. I think the main component of a peaceful and effective protest is some kind of leadership. Someone who can monitor, someone who can say "No, that's not what we do here."

But it has to be in conjunction with the police. It takes both sides to make this work. It takes some willingness on the part of demonstrators and the police to exercise restraint. When you have a large group of people who want to peacefully protest, police should facilitate that. You don't focus your effort on setting up barriers around peaceful protestors and having policemen, with their arms folded, standing in the way. This concentrates police attention on the people least likely to cause trouble and then you don't have any leftover police to catch looters and vandals elsewhere.

> "Where do we go from here? Some
> have cheered the ethical and
> practical benefits of abolition. Others
> have championed the merits of
> certain reforms."

Confusing Messaging Can Threaten a Movement

Michael Javen Fortner

In the following viewpoint, Michael Javen Fortner examines the confusion surrounding the Defund the Police movement, spawned in 2020 by the police killing of George Floyd, unfortunately just one of many murders of Black Americans at the hands of law enforcement. While evidence supports the need for police reform, the term "defund the police" is interpreted in different ways even by its supporters, and with no central leader to define the messaging, the movement could lose steam. Michael Javen Fortner is assistant professor of political science at the Graduate Center, the City University of New York. He is the author of Black Silent Majority: The Rockefeller Drug Laws and the Politics of Punishment.

As you read, consider the following questions:

1. Why do leaders disagree on the strategy of the Defund the Police movement?
2. Which side do most African Americans land on, according to surveys cited in the viewpoint?
3. Which side does the author take?

N ational polls demonstrate that there is a great deal of confusion around the word "defund," and most African Americans see it as something other than completely ridding cities of cops. Most Americans, especially Blacks, see room for community groups and non-law enforcement professionals, such as social workers and doctors, in a broader public safety strategy. The evidence recommends the same.

For seven minutes and 46 seconds,[1] a Minneapolis police officer put his knee on George Floyd's neck, stealing his last breaths. Floyd's callous murder on May 15, 2020, sparked a conflagration across American cities that consumed national attention. "Defund the police," announced former Bernie Sanders presidential campaign speechwriter David Sirota, "has become a nationwide mantra."[2] While pundits wrestled with what that slogan should mean, Mariame Kaba, a prison abolitionist, set the record straight in the *New York Times*: "Yes, We Mean Literally Abolish the Police." George Floyd's murder by a Minneapolis police officer was the rule for her, not the exception: "When a police officer brutalizes a black person he is doing what he sees as his job." Put simply, "We can't reform the police."[3] Similarly, Michelle Alexander, author of *The New Jim Crow*, was not surprised that "growing numbers of people are working to defund the police and reimagine justice," declaring, "The system is not broken; it is functioning according to its design."[4]

Many traditional Black leaders have pushed back against the calls from activists to "defund the police." James Clyburn, U.S. representative from South Carolina and chair of the Democratic

Caucus, was as unequivocal as Kaba: "Nobody is going to defund the police." He explained, "Re-imagine policing…, [t]hat is what we are going to do."[5] Al Sharpton noted: "I don't think anyone other than the far extremes is saying we don't want any kind of policing at all."[6] He later described abolition as an idea "a latte liberal may go for as they sit around the Hamptons discussing this as some academic problem."[7] According to Newark Mayor Ras Baraka, a Black progressive with deep Black nationalist roots, defunding the police is a "bourgeois liberal" solution. Although he seeks "significant reforms," he questions the wisdom of abolition: "Who would respond to calls for service for violence and domestic abuse?"[8] By early July, the African American Mayors Association had drafted a policy blueprint that focused on greater transparency; revising policing-related contracts; changing federal policy; engaging the community; and making budgets "reflect community values."[9] Though it was vague on specifics, McKinley Price, the association's president and mayor of Newport News, Va., made one thing very clear: "We do not call for abolishing or defunding police departments."[10]

How do we break this impasse? Where do we go from here? We can begin to look for a path forward by reflecting on how the politics of punishment have evolved from the 1980s to today, reviewing polling data and key policy moments. While many accounts of attitudes about policing highlight "racial divides,"[11] my analysis seeks to understand African American opinion on its own terms as well as in relation to other racial groups and seeks to capture its political significance historically and in the current moment. Instead of assuming a coherent "Black perspective" on policing and punishment, it centers the complex, and sometimes contradictory, internal politics of public safety within African American communities.[12] While most Blacks have been less punitive than most whites, most Blacks have also been extremely punitive in their own right.

First, African American attitudes grew increasingly punitive towards crime, policing, and punishment in response to rising violence in Black communities from the 1960s to the early 1990s.

The passage of the Violent Crime Control and Law Enforcement Act of 1994 (aka "the crime bill") provides a key example. Anti-crime sentiments made African Americans a crucial member of the "get tough" coalition that defined American politics and policy in that era. Second, crime's stunning denouement lead Black opinion to moderate, as revealed by attitudes and events in New York City as reported violent crimes dropped sharply from their peak in the early 1990s, in part reflecting new policing strategies. Despite living in safer communities and continuing to see police brutality, most African Americans remained committed to effective policing as a public safety strategy. The Black Lives Matter movement emerged, in part, however, as a response to these same policing strategies and signals a major generational division in African American politics.

Third, manifestations of these generational splits were visible in the 2020 Democratic presidential primary campaign and the subsequent protests seeking to "defund the police." Recent surveys show that most African Americans side with Clyburn more than Alexander. Most Americans, including Blacks, endorse meaningful police reforms, but they also oppose abolition, although that is favored by a plurality of Black and white millennials. The fate of defund measures in Minneapolis, Atlanta, and New York City document the ways in which the fight over "defund the police" is as much a conflict between young and old and left and center as it is between Black and white.

My analysis then returns to the central question: Where do we go from here? Some have cheered the ethical and practical benefits of abolition.[13] Others have championed the merits of certain reforms.[14] Without rehashing or adjudicating between these perspectives, one can still see a policy space that heeds the constraints of contemporary attitudes and attends both to the deep and legitimate fear of crime that continues to weigh heavily on many African Americans and to the terror that police violence foments among all Blacks.[15] Living with overpolicing and underprotection,[16] most African Americans seek the reconstruction of public safety strategies, urban communities, and the relationship between those strategies and those communities. We need to end police brutality without ending policing.

Notes

1. "Prosecutors say officer had knee on George Floyd's neck for 7:46 rather than 8:46," Los Angeles Times, June 18, 2020.
2. David Sirota, "There's No Way Around It: Spending on Police in the U.S. Is Out of Control," Jacobin, June 8, 2020.
3. Mariame Kaba, "Yes, We Mean Literally Abolish the Police," New York Times, June 12, 2020.
4. Michelle Alexander, "America, This Is Your Chance," New York Times, June 8, 2020.
5. Chandelis Duster, "Clyburn says he does not support defunding the police," CNN, June 14, 2020.
6. "Rev. Al Discusses Possible Changes to Minneapolis Police Department," Morning Joe, MSNBC, June 8, 2020.
7. Morning Joe, MSNBC, September 12, 2020.
8. Sam Sutton, "Newark Mayor: Dismantling Police a 'Bourgeois Liberal' Solution for a Much Deeper Problem," Politico, June 11, 2020.
9. African American Mayors Association, Inc., Black Mayors Release Pact on Police Reform (Press Release), June 30, 2020.
10. Tom Jackman, "African American mayors lay out plan for police reform without 'defunding,'" Washington Post, July 27, 2020.
11. Nazgol Ghandnoosh, *Race and Punishment: Racial Perceptions of Crime and Support for Punitive Policies* (Washington, D.C.: Sentencing Project, 2014). Mark Peffley and Jon Hurwitz. *Justice in America: The Separate Realities of Blacks and Whites* (Cambridge: Cambridge University Press, 2010).
12. This analytical perspective draws inspiration from the following: Jennifer L. Hochschild, *Facing Up to the American Dream: Race, Class, and the Soul of the Nation* (Princeton: Princeton University Press, 1995); Adolph L. Reed, *Stirrings in the Jug: Black Politics in the Post-Segregation Era* (Minneapolis: University of Minnesota Press, 1999); Cathy J. Cohen, *The Boundaries of Blackness: AIDS and the Breakdown of Black Politics* (Chicago: University of Chicago Press, 1999); Lester K. Spence, *Knocking the Hustle: Against the Neoliberal Turn in Black Politics* (Brooklyn: Punctum Books, 2015).
13. Alex S. Vitale, *The End of Policing* (Verso Books, 2017).
14. Robert Muggah and Thomas Abt, "Calls for Police Reform Are Getting Louder—Here Is How to Do It," Foreign Policy, June 22, 2020.
15. Michelle Alexander, *The New Jim Crow: Mass Incarceration in the Age of Colorblindness* (New York: New Press, 2012).
16. Jill Leovy, *Ghettoside: A true story of murder in America* (New York City: Spiegel & Grau, 2015).

> *"Instead of relying on the usual*
> *methods of political insurrection,*
> *[Gandhi] found another:*
> *self-sacrifice of an intensely*
> *personal kind."*

Charismatic Leaders Can Be Effective, but They Need the Consent of the Movement's Rank and File

Clifton B. Parker

In the following viewpoint, Clifton B. Parker discusses the work of two scholars who have studied India's nonviolent independence movement and Mahatma Gandhi's role in keeping that movement peaceful. The author argues that without the right kind of leadership, movements that start out nonviolent can quickly become violent. In order to avoid this, leaders need to select the right followers. At the time this was written, author and journalist Clifton B. Parker was director of communications at the Stanford News Service.

"Gandhi's Nonviolent Approach Offers Lessons for Peace Movements, Stanford Scholar Says," by Clifton B. Parker, Stanford University., October 29, 2014. Reprinted by permission.

As you read, consider the following questions:

1. What did Gandhi do to avoid having his movement co-opted by those who would use violence for short-term gain?

2. How was self-sacrifice used as a motivating tool in Gandhi's movement?

3. How did Gandhi choose his followers?

The organizational innovations behind Mohandas Gandhi's nonviolent movement in India offer lessons for contemporary peace movements, a Stanford scholar argues.

In a new paper that reinterprets Gandhi's legacy, Stanford's Saumitra Jha, an associate professor of political economy, examines the potential and pitfalls of nonviolent disobedience. His co-author is Rikhil Bhavnani, an assistant professor of political science at the University of Wisconsin-Madison.

Too often, nonviolent civil disobedience fails, they wrote. "The key lesson of India's successful movement is sometimes reduced to the simple but rather unhelpful admonition, 'Find another Gandhi,' who can lead through individual charisma," Jha said in an interview.

The truth is more complicated—and besides, India's independence movement took decades and experienced plenty of ups and downs, he added. For Jha and Bhavnani, this was fertile ground to study what worked and what did not.

The scholars researched numerous data sources on India's independence movement, including voter turnout, intelligence reports, archival correspondence and records from both India and Britain. They also examined the effectiveness of 250 nonviolent and violent political campaigns globally between 1945 and 2006.

The problem with movements that begin nonviolently is that they can be co-opted by people prone to exploit the short-term gains that violence offers, the two wrote. To overcome this, Gandhi mobilized followers across ethnic and societal lines, and elevated leaders and followers truly committed to nonviolent aims.

Indian Innovations

Timing was also crucial, Jha said. The global Great Depression of the early 1930s gave impetus in India for political coalitions to be formed. Farmers and agriculturists were swayed to join with Gandhi's reformers in the Civil Disobedience Movement of 1930-1932, as it was known. This came in the wake of Gandhi's reforms of the Indian Congress in the 1920s that opened the political system to people who were committed to nonviolent objectives and tactics.

"These organizational innovations took the (Indian) Congress movement from one dominated by a rich elite to one organized on the principle of self-sacrifice, selecting future leaders who could be trusted to maintain non-violent discipline in pursuit of the extension of broad rights and public policy objectives," Jha and Bhavnani wrote.

This yielded results. The British finally decided to negotiate, and by 1936 allowed both local autonomy and the first broadly democratic elections in India, according to the researchers.

It was also the people—leaders and members—who galvanized the peace movement and made it more successful than other campaigns, both in India and elsewhere, they said.

"Addressing these challenges for sustaining a nonviolent movement requires identifying and mobilizing sufficient numbers of select potential followers that are willing to forgo temptations for violence in favor of national objectives," Jha and Bhvanani wrote.

How did Gandhi find the right people? Jha said the iconic Indian leader's legendary requirements of "self-sacrifice"—for himself and his followers—were instrumental in separating out those who did not believe in peaceful resistance. Indeed, those who courted arrest for civil disobedience and faced hard labor in British jails revealed their trustworthiness and authenticity. Many veterans of India's jails subsequently advanced to leadership ranks.

In contrast, the Indian independence movement lacked such fortitude at other times, according to Jha. For example, the British arrest of 60,000 Congress leaders in an overnight sweep in 1942 led to a rapid breakdown of nonviolent discipline.

"Nowadays, Indian politicians also go to jail a lot, but for very different reasons than during the independence movement," said Jha, referring to the political corruption of today's India.

Gandhi was especially astute in reorganizing the movement away from elite politics on one hand and religious zealotry and terror on the other.

Instead of relying on the usual methods of political insurrection, he found another: self-sacrifice of an intensely personal kind. And in doing so, he and his followers revealed the strength of what happens when a mass mobilization is committed to nonviolent methods and big-picture public objectives.

Broader Applicability

Jha said Gandhi's lessons for reform are not India-specific—they offer lessons for freedom movements around the world. He and Bhavnani found that large nonviolent campaigns that exceed 500,000 members—while attracting intense international media attention—are likely to be most effective in achieving change.

However, without organizations that maintain nonviolent discipline, such mass movements often turn violent, they said.

Audiences are important, too. In the case of Gandhi, the international media, particularly in America, showed that coverage could impose costs on entities like Great Britain that might otherwise benefit from the violent repression of nonviolent movements.

Jha and Bhavnani point to the intrinsic link between nonviolent movements and the success of new democracies.

"Unlike leaders that condone violence and can thus punish others using violence, nonviolent leaders both need a mass movement to be successful as well as the consent of the movement's members," they wrote. And large-scale consent is the legitimacy upon which democracies are based.

Jha said the research may help explain why nonviolent movements like India's have led to democratic consolidation, while democracies have often faltered in other places that lacked more enduring nonviolent commitments and leadership.

> "The martyrdom in Seattle conforms,
> in Trujillo's photograph, to the deep
> religious roots of the idea of suffering
> for a cause."

Silent Imagery Can Be as Powerful to a Movement as Galvanizing Speakers

Jonathan Jones

In the following viewpoint, Jonathan Jones argues that the use of powerful imagery can motivate protesters and also can bring attention to the causes of social movements. Historical examples of this can be found in several famous newspaper photographs during the civil rights movement in the United States, which served to educate the public and change popular opinion. In this case, Jones has found the Occupy Wall Street movement's "iconic image of martyrdom," a photograph of an elderly Occupy protester that resembles a Christian Renaissance painting. Jonathan Jones is an art critic who writes for the Guardian.

As you read, consider the following questions:

1. Jones describes Rainey as "suffering for a cause." Why does that make a powerful statement to fellow protesters, and more importantly, the public?
2. What religious iconography is conveyed in the photograph, according to Jones's interpretation?
3. What examples does Jones give in his warning not to sentimentalize radical politics?

Every nascent political movement needs martyrs. Even the sensible British labour movement, whose history is mostly peaceful and overwhelmingly parliamentary, has its memories of the Tolpuddle Martyrs and the Peterloo massacre. Revolutionary traditions fervently venerate their political saints: Irish republicanism has an especially rich pantheon from Pearse and Connolly to Bobby Sands. The Egyptian revolution, less than a year old, already has martyrs including the artist Ahmed Basiony, who was shot dead by security forces on 28 January, and whose life and work have since been commemorated at the Venice Biennale.

This week the Seattle police provided the Occupy movement a powerful image of martyrdom. Dorli Rainey was not killed—let's not overdo any analogies between economic protests in western democracies and the desperate struggle for freedom in Egypt or Syria. She was "only" pepper-sprayed. But she happens to be 84, and photographer Joshua Trujillo happened to be on hand to take a haunting photograph of her reddened eyes and shellshocked expression that subtly and strongly portrays Rainey as a modern martyr.

I am not suggesting this lightly. The martyrdom in Seattle conforms, in Trujillo's photograph, to the deep religious roots of the idea of suffering for a cause. Rainey resembles a humiliated Christ in this picture. She is supported by two men, one on either side, who both lower their faces—one has his eyes closed in self-protection, the other wears defensive goggles—in what may be a sensible precaution to avoid getting sprayed themselves, but which also looks like a gesture of compassion, of quiet rage and dignified sorrow. It is at once a real moment—the men shielding their eyes while showing her hurt to the camera—and an image straight out of a Christian Renaissance painting.

The men look disconcertingly similar to the supporters of the dead Christ's tormented body in paintings such as Giovanni Bellini's *The Dead Christ Supported by Angels*. The Bellini painting is a great banner of emotion. Bellini depicts Christ nearly naked, his body frontal and wide, the expanse of his pale chest filling the painting with pity: in a similar way, the men supporting Rainey in this photograph frame her strong, striking face, which seems to grow to fill the scene with injured courage. The men display her political wounds just as Bellini's angels display the spear wound in Christ's side.

America is a religious nation and I can't help thinking that either the people in the picture, or the photographer, consciously or unconsciously reached for an image from the iconography of Catholic faith. No movement, in its early history, recognised the power of martyrdom more thoroughly than Christianity did. Obviously, martyrdom is a Christian concept. To die for the faith, by being pinioned to the ground and beheaded—say—or crucified upside down, was to imitate Christ, to reenact the suffering of a God made flesh. The courage of the early Christian martyrs— fact or fiction—provided the church with a popular repository of heroes, relics, and sacred memories. Not all martyrdoms result in death, so even from a pedantic standpoint, Rainey conforms to the tradition—the arrows that pierce Saint Sebastian in so many paintings did not kill him, for instance.

Trujillo's photograph recreates the image of Christian martyrdom in a modern context in a way that resembles contemporary spiritual artworks such as Bill Viola's videos—yet it happened in the heat of the moment, on the streets of Seattle. This is not a staged photograph, it is real life. And as such it is a warning to the police and political bosses not to create too many martyrs, if they really want Occupy to disappear.

Lest we sentimentalise radical politics too much, let's remember that no political movement guarded the memory of its martyrs more fulsomely than National Socialism did. Or that one of the most potent images of secular political martyrdom, David's painting *The Death of Marat*, elegises a bloody architect of the Terror in the French Revolution. What does seem to be the case, looking at this photograph and its echoes of Christian art, is that from the time of the French revolution in the 1790s down to today, the idea of suffering for a cause has drifted from the declining cloisters of western Christianity onto the streets and the barricades. As they sing in *The Red Flag*: "The people's flag is deepest red/ It shrouded oft our martyred dead."

Periodical and Internet Sources Bibliography

The following articles have been selected to supplement the diverse views presented in this chapter.

Laura Barrón-López, "Why the Black Lives Matter Movement Doesn't Want a Singular Leader," Politico, July 22, 2020. https://www .politico.com/states/new-york/albany/story/2020/07/21 /why-the-black-lives-matter-movement-doesnt-want-a-singular -leader-1302934.

Stephen Chupaska, "Successful Protests Require Diversity and Focus," Columbia Business School, June 15, 2020. https://www8.gsb .columbia.edu/articles/ideas-work/successful-protests-require -diversity-and-focus.

Joshua Keating, "The George Floyd Protests Show Leaderless Movements Are the Future of Politics," Slate, June 9, 2020. https:// slate.com/news-and-politics/2020/06/george-floyd-global -leaderless-movements.html.

Daniel S. Levy, "Behind the Anti-War Protests That Swept America in 1968," *Time*, January 19, 2018. https://time.com/5106608 /protest-1968/.

Van Nguyen Marshall, "South Vietnam Had an Antiwar Movement, Too," *New York Times*, September 15, 2017. https://www.nytimes .com/2017/09/15/opinion/south-vietnam-had-an-antiwar -movement-too.html.

Louis Menand, "When Martin Luther King, Jr. Became a Leader," *New Yorker*, April 4, 2018. https://www.newyorker.com/news /daily-comment/when-martin-luther-king-jr-became-a-leader.

Andrew Roberts, "10 Lessons from History About What Makes a Truly Great Leader," *Time*, October 30, 2019. https://time .com/5713400/10-lessons-history-great-leaders/.

Madeline Schwartz and Erica Sánchez, "Social Movements—and Their Leaders—That Changed Our World," Global Citizen, June 30, 2016. https://www.globalcitizen.org/en/content/movements -social-change-apartheid-civil-rights-suf/.

Maria J. Stephan and Adam Gallagher, "Five Myths About Protest Movements: No, Protests Don't Really Require Charismatic Leaders," *Washington Post*, December 13, 2019. https://www

.washingtonpost.com/outlook/five-myths/five-myths-about
-protest-movements/2019/12/12/700a8afc-1d1d-11ea-87f7
-f2e91143c60d_story.html.

Emily Stewart, "We Are (Still) the 99 Percent," Vox, updated April 30,
2019. https://www.vox.com/the-highlight/2019/4/23/18284303
/occupy-wall-street-bernie-sanders-dsa-socialism.

Neal Ungerleider, "The Stealth Leaders of Occupy Wall Street," Fast
Company, October 7, 2011. https://www.fastcompany
.com/1785698/stealth-leaders-occupy-wall-street.

Malcolm Venable, "Today's Activists Are Harnessing Decentralized
Power, Both Online and in Real Life," Shondaland, March 22,
2021. https://www.shondaland.com/act/a35879432/activists
-embracing-power-the-people.

CHAPTER 4

Has Social Media Helped Make Protest Movements More Effective?

Chapter Preface

S ocial media has been around for decades now, but it's new enough that we're still collecting data and analyzing its effects on various aspects of life. When it comes to protest movements, the jury is definitely still out. Social media has clearly made protests easier to organize, especially in these days of de-centralized leadership of protest movements. Social media was a key ingredient in the Arab Spring protests and in the Occupy Wall Street movement in the early 2010s. A decade later, the protests that erupted after the killing of George Floyd quickly spread around the world via social media, raising awareness of injustice toward marginalized people everywhere, and demanding change. In fact, the Black Lives Matter movement itself began in 2013 as a hashtag campaign.

But it's not clear whether or not social media has been a net win for protest movements. As you will see in the coming viewpoints, many argue that social media is a flawed tool for effecting social change. For one thing, too many marginally connected people tweeting and sharing memes can dilute and even muddy a movement's message. For another, social media is owned and controlled by corporate interests that have the power to decide which messages are disseminated and which are not. These companies are also controlled, at least in some measure, by governments. This can make social media not only less effective, but potentially dangerous for protestors.

These corporations are also motivated by profit, which means their decisions about what messages to boost or share are based not on what is good for society or their users, but what is good for their bottom line. All of these considerations complicate the question of how useful social media is for protesters. One thing is for sure, social media isn't going anywhere, and anyone who hopes to communicate in today's world needs to figure out what to do about it. In the following viewpoints, the authors discuss just that.

*"Roughly eight-in-ten Americans
(79%) say the statement 'social
media distract people from issues
that are truly important' describes
social media very or somewhat well."*

Social Media Can Help Build Movements but Can Also Be a Distraction

Brooke Auxier and Colleen McClain

In the following viewpoint, Brooke Auxier and Colleen McClain break down the American public's responses to poll questions about social media and protest movements. Most Americans say social media can be helpful, but as Auxier and McClain get into the weeds of the study, they find some interesting nuances. Brooke Auxier and Colleen McClain are research associates at the Pew Research Center.

As you read, consider the following questions:

1. Young people are more likely than older people to use social media, but according to this viewpoint, their views about its effectiveness as a tool for social change are less divided. Why do you think that's the case?
2. What are some of the negative aspects of online action, according to this viewpoint?
3. What is "slacktivism" and why is it a problem for social movements that rely on social media?

S ocial media platforms are important for political and social activists. But while most Americans believe these platforms are an effective tool for raising awareness and creating sustained movements, majorities also believe they are a distraction and lull people into believing they are making a difference when they're not, according to a new Pew Research Center survey.

Overall, eight-in-ten Americans say social media platforms are very (31%) or somewhat (49%) effective for raising public awareness about political or social issues, according to the survey of U.S. adults conducted July 13-19. A similar share (77%) believes these platforms are at least somewhat effective for creating sustained social movements.

Smaller shares—though still majorities—say social media are at least somewhat effective in getting elected officials to pay attention to issues (65%), influencing policy decisions (63%) or changing people's minds about political or social issues (58%).

Across political parties, more describe these platforms as effective rather than ineffective when it comes to achieving these goals. Still, there are some partisan differences.

Democrats and independents who lean Democratic are more likely than Republicans and Republican leaners to say social media sites are at least somewhat effective as a way to raise public awareness about political or social issues (86% vs. 74%), create sustained social movements (82% vs. 73%) and get elected officials to pay attention to issues (71% vs. 59%). Partisan gaps are more modest when it comes to these platforms' effectiveness at influencing policy or changing people's minds.

Democrats also stand out as seeing social media platforms as very effective for raising awareness: 39% of Democrats say social media are very effective at this, compared with 22% of Republicans.

While younger Americans are more likely than their older counterparts to use some social media platforms, there are few age-related differences in views of these sites' effectiveness for political engagement—and party differences persist even among younger adults for some goals. For example, 87% of Democrats ages 18 to 29 say social media sites are at least somewhat effective for raising awareness, compared with 76% of Republicans in the same age group. Democrats ages 18 to 29 are also more likely than their Republican counterparts to say these sites are at least somewhat effective at creating sustained social movements (84% vs. 74%) and getting elected officials to pay attention to issues (72% vs. 60%).

Leading up to the presidential election, social media platforms have played a role in raising awareness about voting issues, spreading information about the presidential candidates and allowing users to engage in online activism and campaigning. But when asked about social media's broader impact on political discourse, there are some signs that Americans think these platforms can have both positive and negative effects.

On the more positive side, about two-thirds of Americans say the statements "social media highlight important issues that might not get a lot of attention otherwise" (65%) and "social media help give a voice to underrepresented groups" (64%) describe social media very or somewhat well. Half of Americans also say the statement "social media make it easier to hold powerful people accountable for their actions" describes these platforms at least somewhat well.

But even larger shares of the public think these platforms are distractions and that people may be engaging in "slacktivism"—a term critics have used to describe activism online. Roughly eight-in-ten Americans (79%) say the statement "social media distract people from issues that are truly important" describes social media very or somewhat well, while a similar share (76%) say the same about the statement "social media make people think they are making a difference when they really aren't."

Democrats are more likely than Republicans to see positive impacts of social media. For instance, three-quarters of Democrats say the statement "social media highlight important issues that may not get a lot of attention otherwise" describes these platforms at least somewhat well, compared with 55% of Republicans.

Democrats are also more likely than Republicans to say these platforms help give a voice to underrepresented groups (75% vs. 52%) and make it easier to hold powerful people accountable for their actions (60% vs. 40%).

By comparison, there is more partisan agreement when it comes to some negative aspects of using social media platforms for political engagement. However, Republicans are a bit more likely than Democrats to believe that social media distract people from issues that are truly important (82% vs. 77%) or make people think they are making a difference when they really aren't (80% vs. 74%).

Younger Americans tend to have a more positive outlook about the societal impact of social media. But as with political engagement, partisan differences still exist within the youngest age group. For instance, 70% of Democrats ages 18 to 29 say social media make it easier to hold powerful people accountable for their actions, compared with 49% of Republicans in the same age group. Young Democrats are also more likely than their GOP counterparts to say social media help give a voice to underrepresented groups (82% vs. 63%) and highlight important issues that might not otherwise get attention (79% vs. 64%).

Americans' views on some of these issues are statistically unchanged since 2018, the last time the Center asked these questions. For example, there has been no notable change in people's views about social media helping to give a voice to underrepresented groups, highlighting important issues and distracting people from important issues.

Still, there has been modest change when it comes to the perception that social media make it easier to hold powerful people accountable for their actions. Half of Americans now say this, down from 56% in 2018. At the same time, there has been an uptick in the share of Americans who say social media platforms are making people think they are making a difference when they really aren't, from 71% in 2018 to 76% in the new survey.

Some of these changes persist when looking at partisan affiliation. The share of Republicans who say social media make it easier to hold powerful people accountable for their actions has dropped from 51% in 2018 to 40% today, while views are unchanged among Democrats. Meanwhile, Democrats have become slightly more likely to say social media make people think they are making a difference when they really aren't (+7 percentage points), while Republican views are more consistent across years.

> "Currently, the algorithms underlying
> social media platforms' business
> model amplify the angry and divisive
> voices that drive engagement,
> pushing users towards ever more
> extreme content."

Social Media Can Be Used for Social Good but Is More Often Used to Drive Conflict

Simone Bunse

By now there is little doubt social media can be—and has been— used as a tool to seed hatred and foment violence. However, in the following viewpoint, Simone Bunse argues that it can also be useful for understanding how conflict emerges, making it easier to counter extremism. The author suggests methods for using social media to build peace rather than to spread conflict. Simone Bunse is a content manager for the Stockholm Forum on Peace and Development at the Stockholm International Peace Research Institute in Stockholm, Sweden.

As you read, consider the following questions:

1. What four recommendations does this viewpoint offer?
2. What are some examples of how social media has been used for peaceful protest and to support democracy?
3. How can well-meaning social media campaigns inflict harm?

Human rights activists have used social media technology to organize peaceful protests and defend democracy for more than a decade. More recently, peacebuilders have discovered it can be a tool to understand conflict dynamics and counter extremism better. Yet the potential of social media as a megaphone for promoting human rights, democracy and peace is overshadowed by its dismal record of being used to drive radicalization and violence through disinformation campaigns. This "online frontline" will continue to be the case, unless regulators, social media firms and citizens revisit current policies and practices.

At the 2021 Stockholm Forum on Peace and Development, researchers, policymakers, tech companies and civil society organizations had an opportunity to explore how social media can be harnessed for peacebuilding purposes and to assess policy responses to harmful online disinformation campaigns. This Topical Backgrounder is inspired by these discussions, particularly on the Janus-faced nature of social media. It makes four recommendations—one each for peacebuilding practitioners, policymakers, social media companies and citizens—to protect peace, democratic institutions and people's welfare:

- Peacebuilding practitioners should systematize the use of social media technology for conflict stakeholder analysis, early warning, counter-messaging and the defence of democracy and human rights;
- Policymakers should stem harmful social media disinformation campaigns by creating effective oversight and strict data management guidelines;

- Tech companies should redesign their social media tools to prevent them from being employed for harmful political ends and from favouring conflict over consensus; and
- Citizens should improve their resilience to disinformation, but also demand insight into the information collected about them by social media firms, how it is used and by whom.

Social Media as a Peacebuilding Instrument

Participants in the Stockholm Forum sessions highlighted four uses of social media technology in peacebuilding research and practice: conflict stakeholder analysis; early warning; counter-messaging; and social mobilization for peaceful protest and democracy. However, none of the four uses has yet fulfilled its potential.

Conflict Stakeholder Analysis

Peace and conflict researchers increasingly examine social media content to map conflict actors, trace the links between them and identify their local support networks. This has greatly improved the understanding of Nigeria's Boko Haram, for example, which has relied on social media for its messaging since 2009.

Early Warning

Researchers also monitor social media content to gain better insights into local grievances—a key driver of violence. In sub-Saharan Africa, for example, local grievances have provided a fertile ground for the expansion of extremist groups. Tracking such grievances online in real time can feed into early warning systems for conflict.

Counter-Messaging

Young peacebuilders use social media platforms to develop viable counter-messages to extremists. These are more likely to be successful if grounded in local (sometimes high-risk) in-person activities or activism.

Social Mobilization for Peaceful Protest and Democracy

Social media technology has also created opportunities for people to mobilize politically in defence of democracy and human rights. In 2009 in Moldova, for example, young people relied on Twitter to oppose the country's communist leadership. In Iran, citizens used Twitter to organize protests against the results of the 2009 presidential election, leading to calls for Twitter to be considered for the Nobel Peace Prize. During the Arab Spring in 2011, protestors in Egypt and Tunisia took to social media platforms to organize, spread their message internationally and ultimately overthrow dictatorial regimes. Particularly in repressive regimes, social media has been a communication channel for people to stand up for human rights or share evidence of human rights abuses thereby preventing government monopolization of information. It is hence no coincidence that social media giants, such as Facebook, Twitter and YouTube, are blocked in China, Iran and North Korea.

All four uses of social media could be employed a lot more strategically to reap benefits for peacebuilders or human rights activists. To date, much of the hope connected to social media as a tool for human rights, democracy and peace after the 2009 "Twitter revolutions" has subsided or been replaced with concern about its potential to contribute to conflict.

Social Media as a Driver of Conflict

In the worst cases, social media platforms have been used to suppress internal dissent, meddle in democratic elections, incite armed violence, recruit members of terrorist organizations or contribute to crimes against humanity, as in the case of persecution of the Rohingya in Myanmar. In 2020 there was evidence of social media manipulation in 81 countries and of firms offering "computational propaganda" campaigns to political actors in 48 countries. While propaganda is not new, the 2021 Stockholm Forum highlighted some of the reasons why propaganda on social media presents distinct challenges compared to traditional media, unintentionally drives conflict or affects peacebuilding efforts.

From News Editors to Tech Companies

The rise of news distribution and consumption via social media platforms has shifted the gatekeeping power for information dissemination from editors and journalists—bound by professional codes of ethics, principles of limiting harm and editorial lines—to tech companies owing allegiance primarily to their shareholders. Professional news outlets across the globe now "compete with content producers—domestic and international—who produce junk news that is sensational, conspiratorial, extremist, and inflammatory commentary packaged as news." Social media providers are currently protected against liability for user content and have shied away from becoming "arbiters of truth."

Creation of Echo Chambers

To maximize profit by growing user engagement and participation, social media companies have created sophisticated tools which filter information and place people in virtual echo chambers. These confirm or even radicalize the users' world views. Currently, the algorithms underlying social media platforms' business model amplify the angry and divisive voices that drive engagement, pushing users towards ever more extreme content.

Voter Manipulation and Offline Violence

The pigeonholing of information not only shapes people's world views, but also their behaviour. The violent storming of the United States Capitol Building in January 2021 was, in part, motivated by the false widespread claim that the 2020 election was rigged. Stockholm Forum speaker Aws Al-Saadi, the founder and CEO of Tech4Peace—a large fact-checking network in the Middle East and North Africa—explained how online rumours can kill and fake online news about specific people in Iraq has sometimes prompted others to take justice into their own hands. Maria Ressa, CEO of online news outlet Rappler in the Philippines, argued: "Social media has become a behaviour modification system. And we've become Pavlov's dogs that are experimented on in real time. And the consequences are disastrous."

Interference in Conflict Dynamics

It is also increasingly clear that even well-meaning global social media campaigns can interfere in conflict dynamics. A recent article explained how, after an information leak, the international #BringBackOurGirls social media campaign to free the high-school girls kidnapped by Boko Haram in Chibok in 2014 hindered rescue attempts and may have encouraged the group's growing reliance on gender violence and kidnapping for international attention and ransom.

Risks to Peacebuilders and Humanitarian Efforts

Another prominent theme in several Stockholm Forum discussions was the risk that adverse social media reactions pose to peacebuilders or humanitarian efforts. For example, individuals working in projects with colleagues from countries considered to be adversaries (Armenia/Turkey; Armenia/Azerbaijan) cancelled their participation in these collaborations after suffering personal attacks on social media. Systematic online campaigns to defame humanitarian organizations are another example. Between 2013 and 2017, hundreds of humanitarian White Helmet volunteers were killed in Syria after manufactured social media claims that they were terrorists with links to al-Qaeda and the Islamic State.

Policy Responses to Social Media Disinformation Campaigns

Policy efforts to stem social media disinformation fall into different categories: punitive approaches; voluntary codes of conduct; and resilience building (for example through task forces that identify influence campaigns, fact-checking initiatives and digital literacy campaigns). Punitive approaches criminalize the creation of disinformation. They have been favoured by non-democratic countries that have frequently used them to censor the media or arrest journalists and opposition activists (for example in Belarus, Egypt or Kazakhstan). Voluntary codes of conduct and investment in resilience building and digital literacy have been the policies preferred by democracies that value the protection of free speech (for example Australia, Canada, European Union (EU) member states or the USA).

Multilateral Initiatives

Two codes of conduct by the EU stand out among multilateral initiatives to stem harmful social media use and disinformation. Agreed in 2016 between the European Commission, Facebook, Twitter, Microsoft and YouTube, the EU Code of Conduct on Countering Illegal Hate Speech Online seeks to ensure that "online platforms do not offer opportunities for illegal online hate speech to spread virally" and to counter terrorist propaganda by "expeditiously" removing illegal online hate speech. Since then, numerous other social media providers have signed up. The last progress report showed that companies are, on average, "assessing 90% of flagged content within 24 hours" and "removing 71% of the content deemed illegal hate speech."

In May 2021, the European Commission issued guidance to strengthen the implementation and monitoring of its 2018 Code of Practice on Disinformation—a self-regulatory instrument to commit online platforms and advertisers to countering the spread of online disinformation. The strengthened code of practice contains stronger measures to disincentivize the purveyors of disinformation, increase transparency of political advertising, tackle manipulative behaviour, empower users, and call for improved collaboration with fact checkers and access to data for researchers. A critical next step is to embed it in the EU's Digital Market Regulation. Daniel Braun, deputy chief of staff to Vera Jourova, vice president of European Commission for Values and Transparency, explained during the Stockholm Forum that the aim "is not to regulate content, but rather to ensure that the platforms put in place resources and processes needed to protect public health, democracy, and fundamental rights."

Social Media Company Responses

Content moderation. In line with voluntary codes of conduct, social media companies have removed content, monitored conflict situations, reduced the visibility of certain content or limited the re-sharing of news, and created early-warning systems in partnership with local fact-checking organizations. Between January 2019 and November 2020, for example, Facebook took down more than 10,893 accounts and 12,588 Facebook pages. To monitor conflict situations across the world, the company invested in local language technologies to help flag hate speech. The most recent estimates by Facebook Director of Human Rights Miranda Sissons, suggest that hate speech has fallen to approximately 8 per 1,000 messages.

Corporate human rights policies. In March 2021, Facebook adopted a human rights policy meant to adhere to the United Nations Guiding Principles on Business and Human Rights. The policy commits Facebook to the publication of an annual report on human rights interventions undertaken, starting a fund for offline assistance to human rights defenders and journalists, removal of verified misinformation and rumours, partnership with human rights organizations and continuing technological advancement in early warning prioritization of at-risk countries. Whether other companies follow suit remains to be seen.

Towards context-sensitive algorithms? Tests of ways to break through current information bubbles and polarizing content are also under way. Particularly after the 2020 US election and the storming of the US Capitol Building, Facebook experimented with algorithms that favour rational voices and quality sources over polarization and division. However, any changes to the algorithms in the aftermath of the US election were temporary. Facebook did not disclose the results of its experiment. Although employees reported "nicer news feeds" and a spike in the visibility of mainstream media publishers, the impacts of the revised algorithms are not public. Miranda Sissons said at the Stockholm Forum that Facebook is "actively seeking to invest in and develop the technology that limits the distribution of hateful or policy violating content or content that otherwise defies human rights principles."

Civil Society Organizations' Responses

Civil society organizations have relied on building partnerships to stem disinformation. As an example, in the wake of the Covid-19 infodemic, local fact-checking organizations and local health organizations have partnered with the World Health Organization, the UN and the International Federation of the Red Cross and Red Crescent Societies to launch an initiative to combat dangerous misinformation in Africa. On other occasions, human rights groups have partnered with network analysis companies to monitor digital threats in conflict environments. The collaboration between the Syria Campaign and Graphika, for example, uncovered a concerted disinformation campaign to discredit frontline humanitarian actors and the evidence they collected after Syria's April 2017 sarin chemical attack.

Outlook and Recommendations

Peacebuilders have discovered that social media platforms can be used to research conflict actors, their strategies and grievances. Nevertheless, social media users' track record of employing the technology to incite polarization, extremism or violence casts a deep shadow over social media's potential as a peacebuilding tool. Legislators in democracies and global tech firms are responding to the harmful use of social media technology and systematic disinformation campaigns by adopting codes of conduct, strengthening monitoring and oversight, and collaborating with non-governmental organizations (NGOs) and civil society actors. Long-term investment by national governments is also required to build trust in traditional media and to strengthen civil society's capacity to distinguish fact from fiction. However, progress will be limited if disinformation remains a source of control by autocratic governments and a source of revenue for social media providers. It will also be futile if social media companies' understanding of how technology interferes in local conflict dynamics remains weak.

Although codes of conduct and investment in resilience through digital literacy programmes are promising, self-regulation has had limited effects. To protect peace and stability, democratic institutions, as well as the health and welfare of societies or specific communities, it is crucial for:

- peacebuilding practitioners to use social media technology much more strategically and systematically for analysis of conflict actors, early warning, counter-messaging and the defence of democracy and human rights;
- policymakers to create more effective oversight and data management guidelines to stem systematic disinformation campaigns;
- social media platforms to redesign their tools to prevent them from being employed toward harmful political ends and from favouring conflict over consensus; and
- citizens, civil society groups and researchers to increase their resilience to disinformation, but also demand insight into the information collected about them by social media firms, how it is used and by whom.

> *"Social media, when carefully used, can help citizens in authoritarian countries make their voices heard."*

Social Media Can Play a Successful Role in Protest in Authoritarian Countries

Mike Krings

In authoritarian countries, protesters can face serious consequences—imprisonment or even death—for speaking out against their rulers or state policies. In the following viewpoint, Mike Krings reports on a study that looks to Vietnam for an example of how social media can offer a voice and some protection to protesters. Since this article was written, Vietnam has further cracked down on dissent. Mike Krings is a public affairs officer at the University of Kansas.

As you read, consider the following questions:

1. Why is it so difficult to organize a protest in Vietnam?
2. How did the protesters discussed in this viewpoint avoid setting off a government crackdown in response to their protests about the tree removal?
3. Why did the protesters eventually take their protest offline?

"Study Outlines How Social Media Can Play Successful Role in Protest in Authoritarian Countries," By Mike Krings, The University of Kansas, April 10, 2019. Reprinted by permission.

S ocial media played a central role in the Arab Spring, when citizens demonstrated against and ousted oppressive government regimes. A new study from the University of Kansas analyzes how social media can also help citizens in authoritarian countries oppose state actions without invoking retribution from the government, all by strategically framing their message and sharing information. One such movement even helped state-run media report on and support the cause.

Vietnam is a one-party, authoritarian country in which speaking out against the government and public protest are not tolerated. Yet in 2014, a group of citizens organized a movement via Facebook that called attention to an environmental cause, brought activists together, shared their message, garnered press coverage and ultimately persuaded the government to change its actions. Hong Vu, assistant professor in KU's William Allen White School of Journalism & Mass Communications, co-authored a study that analyzed how the movement was successful.

"Public protests against the government or any challenges to their legitimacy are not allowed in Vietnam," Vu said. "It's very rare, but when people do protest, they can risk their lives, their families, their safety. It's not as easy in Vietnam as it is here to organize a protest. If you're in a group of six or seven people holding signs about anything, you can be arrested. I think, especially in authoritarian countries, social media is greatly changing the way people communicate and get information."

In 2014, government workers in Hanoi began a campaign of cutting down trees in the city. The trees, which were decades old, were slated to be removed because storm season was nearing, according to the government. The first trees were cut down in a busy part of the city, and people noticed immediately and began posting pictures on Facebook, asking for more information. They quickly learned via Facebook, which is hugely popular in Vietnam, that 6,700 trees were slated for removal by the government. Activists quickly formed the group 6,700 People for 6,700 Trees to counter the action. Within 24 hours, the group had more than

9,000 members, much more than planners thought would be necessary to support the movement.

Vu, a native of Vietnam and former journalist in the country, and co-authors Hue Duong of the University of Georgia and Nhung Nguyen, communication manager for Vital Strategies in Vietnam, interviewed 18 activists, participants and journalists who took part in or covered the movement. The study is forthcoming in the *International Journal of Strategic Communication*. The authors found from their interviews and analysis of posts the group was very savvy and deliberate in how it presented its messages, which was vital to avoiding a crackdown from the government. They established a collective identity and invoked emotions, which are crucial to success of any movement. The Facebook group was full of Hanoi citizens who saw the trees as an established, vital part of the community and part of their identities as citizens.

"These activists really knew how to communicate their message on social media, bypass the government and get the mainstream media to follow their message," Vu said. "Ultimately, they got the government to change its plans."

After establishing a collective identity of Hanoi citizens who cared about the trees and how they were part of their lives, they took the movement offline. This step was crucial as they did so without invoking crackdowns on protest and dissent. They began meeting informally to discuss how they could save the trees. Participants deliberately avoided directly criticizing the government, instead focusing on how they loved the trees and wanted to keep them.

The movement was even successful in bringing large groups of people together in public united around a cause. They did so by organizing an "outdoor picnic," in which people talked about their love of the trees, desire to save them and talk only about peace and the benefits of the trees. The government was closely watching them, respondents indicated, but they avoided arrest by sharing positive messages and activities such as group tree hugs and even giving flowers to security forces monitoring the

Social Media as a Tool for Protest

The role of social media in protests and revolutions has garnered considerable media attention in recent years. Current conventional wisdom has it that social networks have made regime change easier to organize and execute. An underlying assumption is that social media is making it more difficult to sustain an authoritarian regime—even for hardened autocracies like Iran and Myanmar—which could usher in a new wave of democratization around the globe. In a Jan. 27 YouTube interview, U.S. President Barack Obama went as far as to compare social networking to universal liberties such as freedom of speech. Social media alone, however, do not instigate revolutions. They are no more responsible for the recent unrest in Tunisia and Egypt than cassette-tape recordings of Ayatollah Ruholla Khomeini speeches were responsible for the 1979 revolution in Iran. Social media are tools that allow revolutionary groups to lower the costs of participation, organization, recruitment and training. But like any tool, social media have inherent weaknesses and strengths, and their effectiveness depends on how effectively leaders use them and how accessible they are to people who know how to use them.

Still, the expansion of Internet connectivity does create new challenges for domestic leaders who have proved more than capable of controlling older forms of communication. This is not an insurmountable challenge, as China has shown, but even in China's case there is growing anxiety about the ability of Internet users to evade controls and spread forbidden information. Social media represent only one tool among many for an opposition group to employ. Protest movements are rarely successful if led from somebody's basement in a virtual arena. Their leaders must have charisma and street smarts, just like leaders of any organization. A revolutionary group cannot rely on its most tech-savvy leaders to ultimately launch a successful revolution any more than a business can depend on the IT department to sell its product. It is part of the overall strategy, but it cannot be the sole strategy.

activities. Again, savvy message framing prevented government reprisal, the researchers found.

"They were very creative in how they framed their activities, calling them 'outdoor picnics' or 'tree hugs,'" Vu said. "They didn't actually say anything against the government. To get participants, they had to be as creative as possible. If they had framed it as a protest, people would not likely have taken part because of the danger. They had to think not only about the movement, but about the risks to people."

Activists attempted to stop tree cutting by interfering with the work of those taking them down. They called on people to place signs on the trees with messages such as "I'm a healthy tree, don't cut me," or tie ribbons around the trees across the city. Such actions caught the attention of Vietnamese media, which are state controlled. While the media weren't allowed to directly report on opposition to the government's plan, they did report on related topics to provide information to the public. Some of the popular stories would focus on how tree protection was handled in other countries and environmental movements in other places. That showed media were willing to report on and share the message of social movements as much as they were allowed to in ways that wouldn't invoke censorship.

Ultimately, the movement was successful, as the government scrapped the plan to cut the trees. The campaign was the first successful movement in Vietnam's modern history and shows how traditional and social media co-exist in the country. The findings also show how social media, when carefully used, can help citizens in authoritarian countries make their voices heard.

"Public opposition is there, but without social media, it would be much harder to organize and coordinate a social movement campaign, especially in authoritarian countries," Vu said. "Our findings show social media not only allows better organization, it allows activists to strategically communicate their message in a way that can guarantee the safety and security of the movement."

> *"The virtual world has cultivated a space that has enlightened many about issues of the real world and emboldened them to act offline."*

Social Media Is Changing the Face of Human Rights Activism

Zara Baig

The killing of George Floyd is an example of a local event that very quickly had international reverberations, thanks in large part to social media. In the following viewpoint, Zara Baig explores how social media can not only organize protesters but also can educate people all over the world about current issues. Zara Baig is a freelance writer who specializes in the philosophical foundations and socio-political nature of criminal and human rights law.

As you read, consider the following questions:

1. According to the viewpoint, how did social media help carry the impact of George Floyd's killing around the world?
2. How has social media gone beyond hashtags and tweets when it comes to activism?
3. How does the dissemination of personal stories aid activism?

"How Social Media Is Changing the Face of Human Rights Activism," by Zara Baig, Human Rights Pulse, December 1, 2020. Reprinted by permission.

D igital activism has become increasingly prevalent over the last five years, but its impact over the past few months has been unprecedented. In the wake of viral video footage of police officers unlawfully killing African-American George Floyd this summer, even as real life stood still, the virtual world rallied to create mass socio-political upheaval. The internet-born Black Lives Matter (BLM) movement re-emerged at the forefront of mainstream discourse with new verve, sparking anti-racism protests worldwide.

Social Media, the Black Lives Matter Movement, and Global Impact

The speed and magnitude at which demonstrations were organised and took place was extraordinary, and inherently due to the use of social media. Social media offers the ability to give authentic first-hand accounts of events, and has become a vital way to communicate incidents of injustice that traditional media either omits, or presents with an underlying agenda. In this case, information on how to educate ourselves on black history was broadcast across platforms, along with live footage of demonstrations, acts of defiance, and practical guidance on where and how to safely protest. The BLM movement has galvanized and maintained momentum through impassioned posts and first-hand stories, helping people to understand the significance of the movement and the reasons behind it, as well as the manner in which it has cultivated deeply profound and positive change.

The advantage of online activism is that it has no geographical constraints. Because of this, the impact of the BLM movement expanded massively. In Europe, many took to protest against the disproportionate imprisonment and death in custody of Black people in their own countries. The movement's impact went beyond denouncing blatant racism and raised discussion about how racism has insidiously trickled into different spheres. In the UK, petitions on decolonising the curriculum were widely tweeted. In India, there was pressure to get rid of "fair and lovely" skin lightening cream.

Other human rights issues have also made social media headlines. China's inhumane treatment of the Uyghur Muslims was documented and heavily discussed on Twitter and TikTok in particular. Many users remarked that they would not have been aware of the human rights crisis occurring had they not seen it on social media. The digital generation's attention was captured largely due to the exponential traction that viral TikToks gained online, prompting many to further research the matter and spread awareness.

Sparking Ground-Level Reform Through Social Media Activism

It is important to note that online activism does also go beyond the realm of hashtags and tweets. YouTube videos have proven to be an accessible and effective method of educating people on human rights issues. This is particularly evident regarding the human cost of fast fashion. There are now numerous videos about the human rights issues of the industry, as well as how and where to sustainably shop and thrift. Additionally, the digital age has allowed people to reach out for help and conversely, to offer it to strangers in need. This form of activism was exemplified through lawyers offering free legal advice to refugees through social media and live chats. Such outreach would have been inconceivable even ten years ago, which shows the power that technology has given.

The inherent aim of human rights activism is to advocate for the rights of the oppressed and underrepresented, and to attempt to change political and social discourse. Social media has played an invaluable role in catalysing this process by levelling the playing field and by amplifying the voices of those not given airtime in mainstream media. Whilst human rights activism may accurately conjure up images of immovable, placard-holding protestors, the existence of social media has modernised it. Every demonstration is now founded upon and mobilised by a wave of hashtags, information shared through stories and posts, and the ability to hear an array of voices and perspectives.

As well as coordinating action, social media has most importantly allowed us to engage with first-hand accounts of those undergoing human rights crises. This has been the crux of increased activism, giving a depth and humanity to previous impersonal news of human rights violations. As personal stories about ongoing matters circulate on the internet, outsiders become more connected with the cause. Additionally, by allowing victims of human rights violations to narrate their own accounts of their circumstances, social media has become a tool for victims to independently shift and reclaim stagnant narratives.

Navigating Challenges in Online Activism

On a cautionary note, the rise of digital activism has also shed light on its flaws, from misinformation to performative activism. A prime example of the latter was when masses took to Instagram to post black screens in a show of solidarity with the BLM movement, using the hashtag #blackouttuesday. Upon clicking on the hashtag, a never-ending sea of black squares took up the screen, counteracting any useful information. Big brands have been called out for statements of solidarity made during the peak of the BLM movement, but not implementing genuine action—such as diversifying their leadership teams, recognising unconscious bias within the company and the hiring process and donate to causes committed to bettering the movement. This conveyed the redundancy of online activism if—albeit well-intentioned—it does not translate into tangible action. Such engagement does little to propel a movement forward. Misinformation in the cyber sphere is also pressing, since anyone can state anything on the internet and baselessly deem it fact. This can and has manipulated socio political discourse and caused serious damage to various movements, with the most prominent example being the way misinformation was shared and exacerbated at an alarming rate during the US elections, proving social media activism is still a work in progress.

A Vital Starting Point for Activism in the 21st Century

Ultimately, social media's unwavering presence in the modern world has contemporised human rights activism and granted it an unparalleled access. The key to incurring change remains the same—implementation on the ground. The virtual world has cultivated a space that has enlightened many about issues of the real world, and emboldened them to act offline. While no system can be entirely reformed with collective clicks, the events of the last few months—across the globe—have perhaps proven it is a legitimate and valuable starting point.

> "The solution to the issue of profit-driven, algorithmic or government-imposed censorship of activists on centralized platforms lies in embracing decentralized alternatives."

Corporate-Owned Social Media Can Be Dangerous for Activists

Jonathan DeYoung

We've seen in previous viewpoints that de-centralized leadership and the use of social media can protect protesters from crackdowns by authority. In the following viewpoint, Jonathan DeYoung points out how social media can be dangerous as well—specifically when it is owned by corporations that collect user data. The answer, the author argues, is decentralized tech. Jonathan DeYoung is a writer, editor, and community engagement veteran with experience in crypto and blockchain.

As you read, consider the following questions:

1. In addition to shareholders, what other groups must corporations answer to, according to the author?
2. What are the dangers of leaving a metadata footprint?
3. According to the viewpoint, what are the requirements for a censorship-resistant communications platform?

"Decentralized Tech Can Protect Activists from Social Media Crackdowns," by Jonathan DeYoung, Cointelegraph, June 17, 2020. Reprinted by permission.

The protests in the United States against police brutality and systemic racism sparked by the murder of George Floyd by former Minneapolis police officer Derek Chauvin on May 25 are showing no signs of stopping.

Rallies and marches have continued in many cities for three weeks now, with events organized in all 50 states as well as in at least 40 countries around the world. Another killing of an African American man in Atlanta, Rayshard Brooks—who was shot in the back twice while fleeing police—has only fed more fuel to the fire.

Most events have been organized and promoted using centralized, corporate-owned social media platforms such as Facebook, Instagram and Twitter. The ease of communication and ability to connect with one another that these large platforms provide have been a major driving force in enabling the activists to mobilize quickly and successfully.

As cities and states begin to unveil policing reforms in response to the widespread protests, with the Minneapolis City Council going so far as voting to disband its police department, privacy advocates have argued that those who are serious about resisting censorship and government surveillance should be wary of centralized platforms because they are controlled, for-profit entities and are subject to coercion from governments. Instead, they point to decentralized technologies and platforms as having the potential to be a safer way for activists to communicate.

Centralized Social Media Presents Risks

As of 2019, an estimated 72% of all U.S. adults use social media, and given the coronavirus-related lockdown, people have been more connected than ever. Organizers of the Black Lives Matter movement have relied on Instagram's "stories" feature to notify protest attendees of location changes, while police scanner apps were downloaded during the initial days of the protests by hundreds of thousands of people, many of whom have taken to Twitter to assume "scanner duty" and broadcast the movements of police officers for protesters.

These platforms give activists and dissidents an unprecedented ability to communicate and organize, but they are run by for-profit corporations that are ultimately beholden to shareholders and governments. This, privacy advocates argue, represents a fundamental flaw in their ability to be secure and resistant to censorship.

Matthew Hodgson, a technical co-founder of the decentralized Matrix communications protocol, told Cointelegraph that these platforms do not serve end users because their business models are to present regular users with ads. In order to best deliver ads, they collect large amounts of user data that accumulates and is at risk of being abused.

Since social media companies are also privately owned entities, they can revoke a user's access to their platforms for any reason, especially if they are seen as too controversial or "non-mainstream," pointed out Bruce Schneier, a security technologist and author. Those decisions affect speech, assembly and the ability to organize, he said, adding: "That's a very dangerous kind of system to pin democracy on."

Oftentimes, the decision to remove a user or their content is made by underpaid content moderators in developing countries or by an algorithm, rather than a company's leadership. Cointelegraph itself found its recent Bitcoin (BTC) halving event canceled by YouTube mid-livestream for being "harmful content."

Sharon Bradford Franklin, the policy director of think tank New America's Open Technology Institute, told Cointelegraph that algorithmic decisions often result in "discriminatory targeting of messages, amplification of harmful content, or silencing of marginalized communities," and that platforms have a responsibility to "take steps to audit and modify their algorithms, and avoid suppressing protest movements."

Centralized Companies Are Beholden to Governments

Shareholders are not the only group that corporations must answer to. These global organizations are also required to follow the laws of the nations in which they operate and can face intense pressure to censor content governments deem subversive. The messaging app Telegram has been banned in Russia since 2018, China's "Great Firewall" blocks access to thousands of websites, and even the video conferencing platform Zoom admitted to deactivating U.S.-based accounts on behalf of the Chinese government.

President Donald Trump suggested on May 27 that the U.S. government could implement a similar approach and ban specific apps or websites that are used by activists to dissent and organize protests. Trump then acted on the suggestion by signing an executive order seeking to remove existing protections that shield social media companies from lawsuits.

Luke Stokes, the managing director of the Foundation for Interwallet Operability and a witness for the Hive blockchain—a decentralized social network—told Cointelegraph that as the U.S. has gotten away with doing many things never thought possible, it would not surprise him if the nation's government took intentional action to censor online platforms. However, doing so would be a slippery slope toward the erosion of citizens' rights, he explained:

> Any form of restricting freedom of speech is dangerous because it is the right that enables us to communicate the reality of every other right. When those with a monopoly on the initiation of force control the narrative, that is a very dangerous thing for a free people.

According to Franklin, however, the even bigger risk is that officials might try to ban end-to-end encryption and force tech companies to weaken the security of their products. Franklin was referring to Republican Senator Lindsay Graham's introduction of the Eliminating Abusive and Rampant Neglect of Interactive Technologies Act, otherwise known as the EARN IT Act, which would effectively ban the use of end-to-end encryption by stripping legal protections from companies that do not comply with a list of government-approved best practices. Yet to be determined, these guidelines are widely expected to include government access to the content of all messages. Franklin told Cointelegraph:

> End-to-end encryption is vital to the ability of activists and ordinary people alike to communicate securely. Particularly as our country confronts police violence and pervasive surveillance, it is critical that people are able to express themselves safely and securely.

While the bulk of organizing has remained public on unencrypted social media platforms, the number of new users downloading the encrypted messaging app Signal has skyrocketed by 259% since the start of the protests. The security-focused app uses end-to-end encryption to protect messages and phone calls, and has long been a favorite of whistleblower Edward Snowden.

However, apps such as Signal that are centrally owned may not be as reliable as some hope. Signal has stated that if the EARN IT Act is signed into law, "it would not be possible for a small nonprofit like Signal to continue to operate within the United States."

Decentralized Platforms May Provide a Solution

Advocates of decentralization argue that the solution to the issue of profit-driven, algorithmic or government-imposed censorship of activists on centralized platforms lies in embracing decentralized alternatives. Indeed, there have been use cases of social movements using decentralized technology to organize.

In Hong Kong, protesters have been using the app Bridgefy to communicate via Bluetooth-based mesh networks that send messages offline, bypassing the Great Firewall and reducing the risk of being shut down. Peer-to-peer mesh networks are composed of individual nodes that all connect into a "mesh." If one node is not directly connected to another, messages will hop from node to node until they reach their intended targets.

In Spain, the Catalan separatist group Tsunami Democratic developed an app built on top of the free software Retroshare, which allows it to create a private, encrypted, peer-to-peer network. New users must scan a QR code of a user that has already joined the network in order to access it. Once instructed, users provide their general geographic location so that they can be activated for regional activities.

Hodgson believes that decentralized communications platforms have the ability to change the way in which social movements are organized. The Matrix communications protocol that he helped develop was designed specifically to be censorship-resistant and give as much privacy and control to each group of users as possible. Hodgson told Cointelegraph:

> It is vital for social movements to be able to communicate privately and without leaving a metadata footprint, otherwise you are simply accumulating data in a centralised messaging service which could be abused, deliberately or otherwise, by that centralised service or the jurisdiction under which they operate.

According to Stokes, in order to be truly censorship-resistant, a communications platform must not only have decentralized hardware but also be decentrally governed. "If there's a single point of failure a government or powerful entity can shut down or censor, then it is not a resilient or censorship resistant system," he said. Stokes believes that decentrally governed blockchain-based platforms have the potential to be the most resilient:

> It's the individuals participating in governance according to the consensus algorithm that give a blockchain censorship resistance. Those could be miners in PoW, stakers in PoS, or voters/stakers in DPoS.

Decentralized Tech for the Bad

There have certainly been a number of instances in which criminal or terrorist groups have used encrypted and/or decentralized technology to facilitate their activities. In 2008, an al-Qaeda-linked group released an app called "Mujahideen Secrets 2"—an update of the original app released in 2007—which promised to be "the first Islamic program for secure communications through networks with the highest technical level of encoding."

In an even more complex operation, the Zeta drug cartel in Mexico kidnapped and enslaved engineers in order to build a do-it-yourself, encrypted, decentralized radio network that relied on hundreds of antennas, signal relay stations and solar power. Most malicious actors, however, opt for existing technologies such as the anonymity-centric Tor browser to host illicit sites on the darknet, often financed through cryptocurrency payments in BTC, Ether (ETH) or Monero (XMR).

The Islamic State group has also experimented with several decentralized platforms including Riot.im, a free, open-source messaging app based on the Matrix protocol that boasts complete privacy. Hodgson—who is also CEO of New Vector, the developing company of Riot.im—said that while it is impossible to stop bad people from using open networks, developers can create tools that allow users to curate content for themselves and filter out anything considered to be bad. He added that the Matrix community is actively building tools into the protocol to facilitate the process.

Everything in society, including "infrastructure, [...] airplanes, cars, restaurants, telephones," can be used for either good or bad, argued Schneier, but "the reason society works is that there are way more good people than bad people." He added that even though privacy-focused technology can be used for nefarious purposes, nations are safer when everyone is secure than when everyone has the same central vulnerabilities.

Technology Is Not a Panacea

While technology may have the ability to allow activists to organize securely and away from the prying eyes of corporations and governments, decentralized and privacy-focused apps should not be considered panaceas. Movements for social change, at their core, revolve around the organization of people. Ross Schulman, the senior policy counsel and senior technologist of New America's Open Technology Institute, told Cointelegraph:

> To the extent that these technologies [P2P and decentralized apps] enable greater abilities for direct and protected communications between people and provide the infrastructure for growing and managing communities, there is the potential for them to influence how social movements grow and spread. With that said, the hard part of organizing is always in the connections that we build with our neighbors in our communities and no technology can replace that if it is missing.

If civil liberties were to deteriorate to the point where activists could no longer organize via centralized platforms without the threat of arrest or death, whether the apps and protocols are centralized or decentralized may not make as big of a difference as some might think. According to Schneier, no piece of software will ever truly protect one against government oppression. "Computer security's not going to save you," he said. "If we actually move into that level of police state, the app will only save you in the movies."

> *"Social media's role in prompting and sustaining social movements cannot be understated, and it highlights the importance of maintaining a free and democratic virtual space."*

Free and Open Social Media Is Crucial to Effective Social Movements

Gabriel Granillo

Clearly social media plays an important, even key, role in today's social protests, but there has been debate about what that role is or should be in order to be both safe and effective for protesters. In the following viewpoint, Gabriel Granillo explores several ways social media can be used, from making use of "low-commitment participants" who might share memes and hashtags but aren't likely to join a protest, to providing a safe digital space for citizens to come together. Gabriel Granillo is an associate editor at the Portland Monthly *in Portland, Oregon.*

"The Role of Social Media in Social Movements," by Gabriel Granillo, SagaCity Media, June 10, 2020. Reprinted by permission.

As you read, consider the following questions:

1. According to the author, what role do low-commitment participants, or "slacktivists," play in social movements?
2. What are the most common ways people join protests, and how does social media help get people into the streets?
3. Why is public ownership of digital spaces essential for building and sustaining social movements?

I t's difficult to imagine a more apt symbol of white privilege than juxtaposing Colin Kaepernick, kneeling silently in protest against systemic racism and police brutality during the national anthem, with Derek Chauvin, a white Minneapolis police officer, kneeling on the neck of George Floyd, a black man, as he gasps for air. What that image doesn't depict is that there were three other officers standing by, or that Chauvin continued to press his knee on the back of Floyd's neck for more than eight minutes while onlookers pleaded with him to let up.

The video of Floyd's killing on May 25 circulated through social media, and since then, formed an uprising, taking the shape of mass protests against police brutality and systemic racism, largely organized online.

In the days that have followed, we've seen handfuls of social media campaigns, including Blackout Tuesday, which, while poised to highlight Black voices, raised concerns that it actually drowned out important information and updates for protesters. Social networks have become hotbeds for liking, commenting on, and sharing information—what some might call "slacktivism"—on local Black Lives Matter protests, guides for folks looking to become allies in the fight against racial injustice, and political debates about race and equality in America. From documenting and sharing unfiltered images and videos of police violence to inciting legislative changes from local leaders, social media's role in prompting and sustaining social movements cannot be understated, and it highlights the importance of maintaining a free and democratic virtual space.

There are a few ways to think about the impact of social media with regard to social movements. The aforementioned "slacktivism" is one, where users circulate information and resources through likes, shares, and retweets. Though it's been disregarded as noncommittal, feel-good politics, there is some evidence that suggests this form of activism can actually help. A study by the University of Pennsylvania Annenberg School for Communication pointed to two significant groups in social protests: a core group and a periphery group. The core group are the users on the street, actively protesting and spreading their message, and the periphery are low-commitment participants, echoing and sharing that message through various social media.

For Kelsy Kretschmer, an associate professor of sociology at Oregon State University, she feels this form of activism has its benefits, coming down on the side of what's known as the "Strength of Weak Ties," which argues that information is most mobilizing when it's coming from acquaintances or a stranger with a common communal background as opposed to a friend, family member, or loved one.

"If you see a lot of people online on your social media feed showing up for a protest, you are also more likely to show up for a protest because you feel like this is what your network is doing, and that can be really valuable," Kretschmer says. "The best predictor of who shows up to protests are the people who were invited, the people who get asked or pressured into going. With social media, that increases the kinds of ways that people can get invited to a protest, even if it's indirectly."

Kretschmer, whose work predominately focuses on social movement organizations, mobilizations, and conflict that arises within groups fighting for social change, says social media can be seen as a tool that works by capitalizing on real-life, or offline, networks that are already mobilizing. In recent protests, including the Arab Spring, the Umbrella Revolution in Honk Kong, #MeToo,

Black Lives Matter, and others, social media has played a key role in amplifying their respective messages, even though each movement arose from very different circumstances and environments.

"The power of images communicates needs in a new way," Kretschmer says, noting that social media's impact right now can be viewed much like the impact of television during the Civil Rights Movement.

"You can see the threads of that happening still. George Floyd's death matters to more people because there was footage of it happening. And it's much different than reading an account in a newspaper," she says. "So social media matters a lot for that, the same way national news broadcasts mattered a lot in the 1960s. That changes how many people are willing to participate."

Floyd's killing is only one name in a long history of police violence against Black people. Since the shooting death of Trayvon Martin in 2012 and the subsequent acquittal of George Zimmerman, BLM has organized thousands of national and international protests and demonstrations.

Christopher Stout, an associate professor in the School of Public Policy at OSU, has been studying the ebb and flow of BLM in the public consciousness and how it's talked about by public officials, and he's currently working on a book about how the movement has shaped discussions about race in American politics. Stout says a large part of BLM's position in the public consciousness is due to how the movement takes shape on social media.

"Between Rodney King and Philando Castile or Mike Brown, police shootings were still occurring, in fact, there's evidence that there haven't been large changes in police brutality over time, it's just that it's finally getting some attention. Social media drives this change," Stout says. "People can hear about something and not think about it, but seeing images on social media and having some of these images go viral, it's really hard to ignore. It's hard to say that these things aren't happening or that these things aren't a problem."

Stout says social media is effective at bringing awareness to certain issues, "but it needs more sustained action. It's just a starting point. Generally, once there's awareness, then you have to go and actually push your politicians to do something about it."

As images and videos of peaceful protests turned awry due to police violence continue to emerge, discussions of significant changes to policy—particularly defunding or abolishing police (including the Portland Police Bureau)—have gained mainstream traction. Portland City Commissioner Jo Ann Hardesty is already proposing to defund specialty police units and transfer more than $4 million "to fund Portland Street Response, a new unarmed, non-police first response option," she wrote on Twitter on June 8.

On Tuesday, June 9, Ted Wheeler announced that the city would dissolve the Gun Violence Reduction Team, PPB transit police, and School Resource Officers, as well as divert $7 million from police and $5 million from other city funds to invest in communities of color.

Our ability to do all of this—raise our voices, organize and activate, share information, demand social and legislative change—is crucial to creating and sustaining a movement, provided we have the physical and virtual space to do that.

How does architecture and community-driven media intersect? Karim Hassanein may help us find the link. He's an Egyptian-American senior marketing coordinator with Bora Architects and President on the Board of Directors at Open Signal, a media arts center in Portland. Spending most of his life outside of the US, Hassanein was studying landscape architecture at University of Oregon during the emergence of the Arab Spring in 2010.

"Watching from afar, here I was studying how built environment is essential to civic well-being and social health and environmental well-being. I didn't want to focus on parks or beautiful back yards for wealthy people. I wanted to know special design applications to meet the demands of revolution in Egypt and to make a more democratic participatory society," he says.

Hassanein was studying how our built environment, particularly cities, can be constructed in order to dictate the actions of people, "the way that we gather or don't gather, the way that we engage with each other and our government or are held at arm's length, the priorities that we place on who gets to develop land and what gets to be built there."

What was emerging in 2011, he says, was virtual space, and in that space, with digital technology and social media, movements and organized action began to take shape. When Egypt began regulating the internet, it got Hassanein thinking about how digital environments, just as our physical environments, can be subject to oversight and control.

When the Federal Communications Commission repealed net neutrality regulations in 2017, it freed internet service providers to block or hinder access as they see fit unless argued against by Congress or the courts. For years, net neutrality advocates have argued that open access to the internet is crucial for innovation and freedom of expression. Hassanein says the BLM movement shows the importance of social media and public, affordable internet access—that without this digital space, our ability to organize and mobilize is severely limited, and he points to projects like Municipal Broadband PDX as potential solutions to a growing fear of regulation.

"The ability to maintain a free, fair, accessible, neutral, virtual space, the ability to have high speed, affordable access for every resident of this country is contingent upon us demanding that our government regulate internet as a utility instead of treating it as this separate issue," he says. "Our ability to use these [digital] spaces for activating and organizing to change our physical environment is largely contingent upon those infrastructures being publicly owned."

Periodical and Internet Sources Bibliography

The following articles have been selected to supplement the diverse views presented in this chapter.

Manal Al Sharif, "The Dangers of Digital Activism," *New York Times*, September 16, 2018. https://www.nytimes.com/2018/09/16 /opinion/politics/the-dangers-of-digital-activism.html.

Joan Donovan, "Trolling for Truth on Social Media, *Scientific American*, October 12, 2020. https://www.scientificamerican .com/article/trolling-for-truth-on-social-media/.

Alexey Gorbachev, "New Generation of Russian Protesters Harnesses Social Media," Voice of America News, February 4, 2021. https:// www.voanews.com/a/press-freedom_new-generation-russian -protesters-harnesses-social-media/6201632.html.

Jane Hu, "The Second Act of Social Media Activism: Has the Internet Become Better at Mediating Change?" *New Yorker,* August 3, 2020. https://www.newyorker.com/culture/cultural-comment /the-second-act-of-social-media-activism.

Yomi Kazeen, "How a Youth-Led Digital Movement Is Driving Nigeria's Largest Protests in a Decade," *Quartz Africa*, October 12, 2020. https://qz.com/africa/1916319/how-nigerians-use-social -media-to-organize-endsars-protests/.

Antonia Malchik, "The Problem with Social Media Protests," *The Atlantic,* May 6, 2019. https://www.theatlantic.com/technology /archive/2019/05/in-person-protests-stronger-online-activism-a -walking-life/578905/.

Aleem Maqbool, "Black Lives Matter: From Social Media Post to Global Movement," BBC News, July 10, 2020. https://www.bbc .com/news/world-us-canada-53273381.

Shira Ovide, "How Social Media Has Changed Civil Rights Protests," *New York Times*, June 18, 2020. https://www.nytimes .com/2020/06/18/technology/social-media-protests.html.

Kalhan Rosenblatt, "A Summer of Digital Protest: How 2020 Became the Summer of Digital Activism Both Online and Off," NBC News, September 26, 2020. https://www.nbcnews.com/news /us-news/summer-digital-protest-how-2020-became-summer -activism-both-online-n1241001.

Bijan Stephan, "How Black Lives Matter Uses Social Media to Fight the Power," *Wired*, November 2015. https://www.wired .com/2015/10/how-black-lives-matter-uses-social-media-to -fight-the-power/.

Cass Sunstein, "Is Social Media Good or Bad for Democracy?" *International Journal on Human Rights*, July 2018. https://sur .conectas.org/en/is-social-media-good-or-bad-for-democracy.

Kayla Zhu, "From Posts to Protests: How Social Media Makes Social Justice Accessible," The Eye-Opener. https://theeyeopener .com/2020/10/from-posts-to-protests-how-social-media-makes -social-justice-accessible/.

For Further Discussion

Chapter 1

1. Which protests in US history have been effective, and which have not? Outline what factors contributed to the success and failure of each.
2. In this chapter, Deborah Doane, an experienced campaigner for a number of issues, argues that the protest movement is failing at least in part because of the focus on anger and calling out evil doers. What ways do you think citizens could demand change without alienating the people they need to persuade?
3. The authors of one viewpoint in this chapter argue that for citizen engagement to be effective and for citizens to have their voices heard, civics needs to be taught in school. Do you agree? In what ways do you think the political process in the United States and Canada might improve if civics were taught more in those countries?

Chapter 2

1. In the viewpoint about civil disobedience in Australia's climate change protests, the author lists several examples of social or political situations that justified civil disobedience. Can you think of others? What injustices would you be willing to risk your liberty to protest?
2. In the viewpoint that related a study on how public opinion responds to violence in protests, people did not increase their support for the opposition when white nationalists were violent but did increase their support for the opposition when antiracists turned violent. Why? Does that response make sense to you? Why or why not?

3. How do you think protesters can avoid responding to heavy-handed policing with violence? What do you think Martin Luther King would suggest to today's protesters struggling with this issue? Do you think his approach is still relevant today? Why or why not?

Chapter 3

1. Oftentimes protests occur because citizens do not feel that their elected representatives are listening to their needs and concerns. How can this happen in a representative democracy, a form of government in which leaders, at least theoretically, depend on the goodwill of the voters to stay in power? Why has this model failed recently? What can be done to change that?
2. This chapter includes an interview with scholar and long-time civil rights activist Clayborne Carson. Dr. Carson remarks that there were no cell phones when he was a young man. How have cell phones changed the power balance between citizens and the police?
3. Many protest movements in some way lead to the election of reactionary governors and presidents, such as Ronald Reagan, Richard Nixon, and Donald Trump. Why does this happen? How can protest movements prevent this backlash?

Chapter 4

1. In the article in this chapter on using social media for peacebuilding, the author writes, "The rise of news distribution and consumption via social media platforms has shifted the gatekeeping power for information dissemination from editors and journalists—bound by professional codes of ethics, principles of limiting harm, and editorial lines—to tech companies owing allegiance primarily to their

shareholders." Can you think of ways society can change this business model?

2. Vietnamese protesters successfully pressured the government to change its policy about tree removal, according to one of the articles in this chapter. Do you think the outcome would have been different if the protest had been about a different sort of policy? Why or why not?

3. Most people give little thought to the business models of the social media platforms they use. However, in this chapter, Jonathan DeYoung points out that tech companies that depend on collecting user data for their profits and are beholden both to shareholders and governments can be dangerous places for protesters to gather or disseminate their messages. DeYoung offers a potential solution. Can you think of other solutions?

Organizations to Contact

The editors have compiled the following list of organizations concerned with the issues debated in this book. The descriptions are derived from materials provided by the organizations. All have publications or information available for interested readers. The list was compiled on the date of publication of the present volume; the information provided here may change. Be aware that many organizations take several weeks or longer to respond to inquiries, so allow as much time as possible.

350.org

PO Box 843004
Boston, MA 02284-3004
email: via website contact form
website: www.350.org

An international movement of ordinary people, 350.org aims to end the age of fossil fuels and ensure climate justice and a sustainable future for all.

American Civil Liberties Union

125 Broad Street, 18th Floor
New York, NY 10001
(212) 549-2500
website: www.aclu.org

The ACLU is an organization that has been working since its founding in 1920 to defend and protect the individual rights and liberties that are guaranteed by the Constitution of the United States.

Black Lives Matter

website: www.blacklivesmatter.com

Black Lives Matter is a social justice movement founded in 2013 in response to the acquittal of Trayvon Martin's killer. Its worldwide mission is to end white supremacy and combat acts of violence against Black communities by the state and vigilantes.

Campaign for America's Future

1825 K Street NW
Suite 400
Washington, DC 20006
(202) 955-5665
email: contact via website form
website: www.ourfuture.org

Campaign for America's Future proposes and promotes new ideas that address the nation's pressing economic and social problems.

Canadian Civil Liberties Association

90 Eglinton Avenue East
Toronto, ON M4P 2Y3
(416) 363-0321
email: mail@ccla.org
website: www.ccla.org

The Canadian Civil Liberties Association is an organization fighting for the civil liberties, human rights, and democratic freedoms of people all across Canada.

Extinction Rebellion

website: www.Rebellion.global

Extinction Rebellion is an international, de-centralized, non-partisan movement. Members use nonviolent actions and civil disobedience to pressure to act with justice on climate and environmental issues.

Fight for Fifteen

email: info@fightfor15.org
website: www.fightfor15.org

The Fight for Fifteen is a global movement of fast-food workers, home health aides, child carers, teachers, airport workers, adjunct professors, retail employees, and underpaid workers everywhere demanding to be paid a living wage for their work.

The Martin Luther King, Jr. Research and Education Institute

Cypress Hall D, 466 Via Ortega
Stanford, CA 94305-4146
(605) 723-2092
email: kinginstitute@stanford.edu
website: www.kinginstitute.stanford.edu

The King Institute at Stanford University is the permanent base of the King Papers project and provides education for the community and resources for scholars of Dr. King and the civil rights movement.

National Organization for Women (NOW)

1100 H Street NW, Suite 300
Washington, DC 20005
(202) 628-8669
website: www.now.org

Founded in 1966, the National Organization for Women is a grassroots arm of the women's movement. NOW is dedicated to many issues and many approaches to fighting for women's rights. It has hundreds of chapters, in all fifty states, and hundreds of thousands of members, many of who are dedicated activists for the cause of women's rights.

TGI Justice Project

370 Turk Street #370
San Francisco, CA 24102
(415) 554-8491
email: info@tgijp.org
website: www.tgijp.org

The TGI Justice Project is a group of transgender, gender-variant, and intersex people fighting against human rights abuses, police violence, racism, and poverty. They seek to create a world rooted in self-determination, freedom of expression, and gender justice.

Zero Hour

email: info@thisiszerohour.org
website: http://thisiszerohour.org

Zero Hour is a youth-led movement offering training and resources for a new generation of climate change activists who want to take concrete action about climate change. Its goal is to protect the rights of the next generation to a clean, safe, and healthy environment.

Bibliography of Books

Marke Bieschke. *Into the Streets: A Young Person's Visual History of Protest in the United States*. Minneapolis, MN: Zest, 2020.

Kevin Boyle. *The Shattering: America in the 1960s*. New York, NY: W. W. Norton, 2021.

Curtis Bunn, et al. *Say Their Names: How Black Lives Came to Matter in America*. New York, NY: Grand Central Publishing, 2021.

Carrie Chapman Catt and Nettie Rogers Shuler. *Woman Suffrage and Politics: The Inner Story of the Suffrage Movement*. Mineola, NY: Dover, 2020.

Frantz Fanon (trans. Richard Philcox). *The Wretched of the Earth* (Anniversary Edition). New York, NY: Grove Press, 2021.

Alicia Garza. *The Purpose of Power: How We Come Together When We Fall Apart*. New York, NY: One World, 2020.

Todd Gitlin. *Occupy Nation: The Roots, the Spirit, and the Promise of Occupy Wall Street*. New York, NY: ItBooks (Harper Collins), 2012.

Peniel E. Joseph. *The Sword and the Shield: The Revolutionary Lives of Malcom X and Martin Luther King, Jr.* New York, NY: Basic, 2020.

Christopher J. Lebron. *The Making of Black Lives Matter: A Brief History of an Idea*. New York, NY: Oxford University Press, 2017.

Michael E. Mann. *The New Climate War: The Fight to Take Back Our Planet*. New York, NY: Public Affairs, 2021.

Vanessa Nakate. *A Bigger Picture: My Fight to Bring a New African Voice to the Climate Crisis*. Boston, MA: Mariner, 2021.

Derecka Purnell. *Becoming Abolitionists: Police, Protests, and the Pursuit of Freedom*. New York, NY: Astra House, 2021.

T. V. Reed. *The Art of Protest: Culture and Activism from the Civil Rights Movement to the Present* (Second Edition). Minneapolis, MN: University of Minnesota Press, 2019.

Kate Robertson and Ella Robertson. *How to Make a Difference*. London, UK: Cassell, 2019.

Stacey K. Sowards. *¡Sí, Ella Puede! The Rhetorical Legacy of Delores Huerta and the United Farm Workers*. Austin, TX: University of Texas Press, 2019.

Greta Thunberg. *No One Is Too Small to Make a Difference*. New York, NY: Penguin, 2019.

Index